TURNAROUND TOOLS FOR THE TEENAGE BRAIN

Helping Underperforming Students Become Lifelong Learners

Eric Jensen and Carole Snider

JB JOSSEY-BASS™
A Wiley Brand

CONTENTS

ABOUT THE AUTHORS

Eric Jensen is a former teacher who has taught students from the elementary level through the university level. Jensen cofounded SuperCamp, the nation's most innovative and largest academic enrichment program, now with nearly sixty thousand graduates. He has authored twenty-six books, including *Enriching the Brain, Student Success Secrets, Teaching with the Brain in Mind, 30 Days to Bs and As, SuperTeaching*, and *Teaching with Poverty in Mind.*

Jensen's academic background includes a bachelor's degree in English and a master's degree in organizational development, and he is completing his doctoral degree. As a leader in the mind and brain movement, Jensen has made over fifty-five visits to neuroscience labs and interacts with countless neuroscientists. He is deeply committed to making a positive, significant, lasting difference in the way we learn. Jensen's public programs are found at www.jensenlearning.com. Currently, Jensen does staff development, conference speaking, and in-depth trainings.

Carole Snider is a former teacher and school counselor from Ohio public schools. Snider's experience includes teaching middle school English and providing counseling services for children from grades K through 12. Snider currently serves on the state governing board for Ohio school counselors, is an adjunct professor, and recently authored the graduate course Succeeding with Students of Poverty. She has organized and facilitated numerous staff development and conference presentations on teaching the whole child, team building, stress management, and raising student achievement for schools across the United States.

Snider holds a bachelor's degree in education and a master's degree in guidance and counseling. She is driven by the belief that every child can be successful, and that schools are honored and have the opportunity to facilitate this success. She is passionate about promoting total fitness—mind, body, and soul—for people of all ages, and continues her research in this area. Carole lives with her husband in Batavia, Ohio. She continues to offer staff development and conference presentations for educators and can be contacted at csnider2@fuse.net.

ACKNOWLEDGMENTS

Eric Jensen

First, we both appreciate our editor, Marjorie McAneny, who approved this project and has provided encouragement and guidance. Further, I am indebted to the scientists, researchers, and editors who made this book happen, including Pam Rooks and Nanette Metz. Finally, I am very grateful for the partnership with Carole, who initiated this book. Her commitment to student achievement has helped drive this effort, and any success is mostly hers.

Carole Snider

I want to give special thanks to all the teachers who have shared their stories of success and sometimes failure with me. Many thanks to Rita for listening to, questioning, and encouraging me throughout this process. I will always be deeply indebted to Eric for his belief in me, and for his continual support in bringing this project to fruition. And a final thank you to my husband, Cliff; two sons, Jeff and Gary; daughter in love, Kathleen; and grandchildren, Tyler, Skylar, JT, and Summer. I could not have done this without you.

INTRODUCTION

This book was born as we worked with teachers across the United States and other countries who shared their deep-seated frustration and anguish in regard to their struggling students. We are grateful for their willingness to open their hearts and reveal to us their desire to do more, to be better. We have seen firsthand the professionalism, hard work, and undying dedication of these teachers as they search for answers to their challenges. We thank them for their commitment and for their ongoing determination to help these students.

Schools can no longer accept the fact that large numbers of students are not graduating, and as a result are more likely to be on their way to economic struggles rather than success and satisfaction. We believe that every student can learn, but perhaps at a different pace or in a different manner compared to other students. We have witnessed schools in which success is for all, not just the select few. We have also observed schools in which the success gap is widening rather than closing. We have seen students who are lethargic, overweight, depressed, angry, and failing academically, and who have poor personal and interpersonal skills. They seem to be simply putting in their time. This is devastating for us because we know it doesn't have to be this way.

Knowing that most teachers are already investing 100 percent–plus in these students, we turned to the research for answers on how to turn the struggling kids around. This book has been several years in the making, which is a short time to work on a topic of this magnitude and significance. What we have written represents a research-based approach to the often overwhelming dilemma of how to help struggling students. We are convinced that applied research can provide the solutions that last a lifetime for these students. Acknowledging the multitude of ways to measure success, we have focused on the short term for current academic success, and have focused equally on the skills students need for lifelong achievement. Often these skills are one and the same, which was encouraging for to discover us as we kept digging for answers. We feel that schools can be positive and powerful places for the struggling student, and that they are the only hope some kids may have.

Dramatic changes are beginning to take place in schools, as educators at all levels embrace the belief that regardless of gender, race, or economic status, every student can excel. It is our heartfelt hope that this book will provide teachers with tools to facilitate these changes further so no student has to live in the richest country in the world and still be poor when it comes to knowledge, opportunities, and life satisfaction.

With over seven thousand secondary students dropping out every day in the United States (Alliance for Excellent Education, 2007), this is a book that needed to happen. The purpose of the book is to reclaim underperforming students and help them graduate. We can all find good reasons to ''pass the buck'' or ''kick the can down the road,'' but the bottom line is this: we must find a way to help kids succeed. The ''annual class'' of students who drop out every year costs the national economy over a third of a trillion dollars over the course of these individuals' lives (Levin, 2005). This is money that comes out of your pocket; every dollar the government has to spend on juvenile justice, welfare, drug wars, criminal justice, and increased health care costs comes out of the same ''big bucket'' of budgets for schools, roads, and law enforcement. We have to keep kids in school and build their competencies, or it is a slippery cultural and economic downhill slope for all of us.

The path in this book is straightforward. You'll be taken on a journey on which you will discover research showing that (1) students' underperformance does not tell you their destiny; (2) brains can change, IQs can change, and attitudes can change; and (3) if you have the will and skill, you can make a significant and lasting difference in more students' lives than you ever thought possible. This book provides that ''will'' by helping you see that reaching the book's objectives is possible. This book helps you find the ''skill'' by showing you specific strategies, websites, and content that will build the academic competencies kids need.

The first chapter, which is all about ''learning for life,'' takes the long-term view. It reminds us to focus on developing skills that are useful over time. Society is changing so fast, your students must become true learners for life. Chapter Two is all about changing the brain. This chapter will show you how to change your students' brains through purposeful effort, not chance. Chapter Three is all about instilling a strong positive attitude in your kids. You'll learn how to promote a winner's mind-set that will ultimately determine a student's level of success throughout his or her life. You'll learn how to teach optimism, and how to develop greater personal accountability in each of your students. Most of all, you'll learn the power of a never-ending growth mind-set so that learning is lifelong. Chapter Four is all about capacity building. We focus on building executive function, which encompasses those critical thinking skills for school and life success. Most important, you'll learn that executive function skills can actually be taught and refined for practical use.

Chapter Five is a gold mine; it's all about fostering student effort. We know that kids who try harder have a better shot at success. This chapter teaches you how to tap into a student's internal motivation as well as how to expand your own toolbox. You'll learn what "drives" kids to try hard in a few short pages. Chapter Six focuses on exceptional learners—kids who are different but not broken. This chapter emphasizes that all learners can be successful, no matter what their current academic situation. But first, you have to learn what the specific signals are that tell you to make serious changes and how to either use "work-arounds" or lasting interventions. To do that, you'll be integrating the "rules" for how the brain changes from Chapter Two in a novel way. They're worth their weight in gold!

Chapter Seven reveals how the mind, body, and soul are synergistically integrated, so you can support the process of student growth. This chapter also explores the role of nutrition in success, the impact of daily thinking habits on learning, and the importance of exercise to achieving a balanced life. The last chapter discusses the process of learning how to focus, which includes using meaningful and appropriate strategies for reaching goals. This chapter identifies steps toward success and shows you how to initiate them among students.

Here's how you might get the most out of this resource. First, browse the book to get a brief overview. That's always a smart practice with any "how-to" book. This book may have some chapters with catchy titles that you're tempted to jump into, but it's written in a linear fashion. That means you are likely to need each preceding chapter to make sense of and get the best use out of the following chapter. In real life, we all have skipped around a book before—but in this case, follow the sequence and you'll develop a powerful understanding of both what the research tells us and how to implement actionable strategies for student success.

One more thing: you know your students best. If you think one of your students is just an insight or a skill away from doing well, you may be tempted to skip around the book and grab strategies here and there. But chances are, if you are reading this book, you'll need more than a pep talk. That's why it's critical, if your challenging student needs a lot of help, to remember this: the brain does not make changes in response to occasional random input. If you provide random services, and you are "on-off" with a fun strategy once a week, no change will happen. You'll need to be a purposeful, focused, relentless, adaptive force in each student's life. If you're willing to be that committed to the student, he or she will become committed to you, too. This book will be your most powerful ally. We know you'll enjoy it; we both welcome you to a new level of student success!

CHAPTER ONE

TEACH STUDENTS TO LEARN FOR LIFE

This student's first memory is of standing in the living room of his house at age two. Tears streamed down his tiny cheeks. That was the day the divorce went through, and his mother was walking out the front door. Four crazy years later, his father remarried for the second of four times. The first of his three stepmothers was violent, abusive, and an alcoholic. Both of his older sisters quickly moved out of the house. One lived with the neighbors, and the other escaped to live in the garage. For ten of his thirteen school years, he was terrorized by his violent stepmother. Blood and broken glass were commonplace in the house. Every time things got *really* bad, the children moved away to stay with relatives or to live on their own. Then his stepmother would promise to be good, and they'd move back. This student lived with his grandmother, with his aunt, with his uncle, then on his own again. The cycle repeated itself every couple of years.

School was a train wreck. He went to nine schools and had 153 teachers. In class, he usually sat in the back and often acted out. He could never do homework; his home environment was a war zone. He had no parental support, and his only friends were even worse troublemakers than he was. He was truant often, arrested twice, and constantly disciplined in high school. He struggled with grades in high school, but finally graduated. His first two years at a local state college were not much better. The drinking started soon after, and things were not looking good. At this stage, would you place a bet on this student to succeed?

WHAT LEARNING FOR LIFE IS ALL ABOUT

We're wondering if you have students who haven't seemed to find their way in school. We also wonder if you have students who seem to struggle every single day you see them. If you do, then you may be interested to know how the student mentioned in the preceding story turned out.

We told you that it's a real story, and it is. It's Eric's own story, and it's the ''G-rated'' version. What's hard for many to believe is that small, targeted interventions made all the difference in Eric's world as a student. Two secondary teachers changed his life. It did not take some monstrous life-changing moment; it took the right things at the right moments. Learning, just like life, is not a sprint. Learning and applying what you learn to life is a constant, ongoing process. This book is about creating a mind-set in your students that *life is not a race*. It's all about putting pieces in place that empower you to become your best self. Never, ever give up on your students; Eric is writing this book today because even though 90 percent of his teachers treated him like an annoyance in their lives, there were two teachers who refused to give up on him. They kept their expectations high while establishing a positive relationship with him. They had total belief in his ability to be and do more, and this belief was exhibited on a daily basis. Will you be that kind of teacher for your kids?

As in Eric's case, the life of a struggling student can be filled with almost insurmountable challenges and disappointment. Eric was one of the fortunate ones. He got the help he needed, academically and personally, and his life changed forever. Many students will not have such a favorable ending to their story without your intervention. There can be countless reasons students struggle, and countless teachers who have worked diligently to help them. You probably are one of those teachers, and would like more answers to that age-old question of how to transform students into true lifelong learners. Here's how this book will empower you to succeed in transforming students daily.

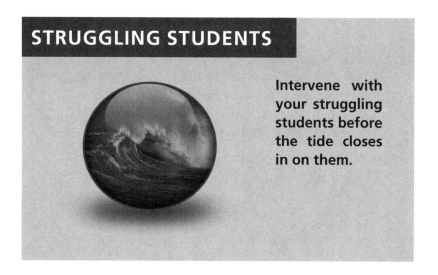

STRUGGLING STUDENTS

Intervene with your struggling students before the tide closes in on them.

THE BIG FOUR

The entire focus of this book is on change. A host of things can change a person's life. In fact, if you read enough, you can get overwhelmed by all the self-help options as well as "teacher help" books out there. But we're going to make it easy. We're going to predict that you know many of the basics already. We're going to assume that you're looking for *what you don't already know*. We're also going to guess that you'd only like to hear about things over which you have a high degree of influence. For example, there's not much you can do about the peers kids hang out with (outside of school) or their parental or caregiver influences. But there are things over which you do have a great deal of influence—and we'll show you what they are. We'll reveal the research and give you specific, easy-to-apply strategies to ensure optimum success for every student, focusing on these "big four" factors that can play a part teens' lives:

> 1. **Attitude**. This factor matters because it influences how much effort students put in as well as their willingness to try diverse learning strategies, and it influences how they think

and feel about their ability to learn. Students with a positive attitude usually go far. The fabulous news is that such an attitude is far more teachable than you thought, and we'll show you how to do it.

2. **Cognitive capacity**. This factor matters because it influences self-esteem, the amount of effort students will invest, the strategies they try, and their attitude. The good news is that every part of cognitive capacity, including attention, memory, processing speed, deferred gratification, and other components, is fully teachable. Students with strong cognitive capacity have a good shot at success, and we'll reveal to you the simple steps to place every student on this positive pathway.

3. **Effort**. The fact is, kids who work hard have a good shot at success. This factor matters because it greatly influences the other three factors listed here. The amazing news is that sustained effort is teachable, and we'll show you how to do it.

4. **Focused strategy**. This factor matters because all the effort in the world won't give you success unless a student is using the right strategy, has the right attitude, and has sufficient cognitive capacity. The stellar news is that focused strategy is teachable, and we'll show you how.

For students to succeed, they'll need to become consummate lifelong learners. The term *lifelong learner* is certainly not a new one, and yet there is a lasting quality to it. Its conciseness, its implications, and its universal use all lend credence to its importance. It can define the difference between a life of mediocrity and one of success. One of the primary benefits of learning for life is acquiring the ability to grow and meet the changes and challenges that are ever present at any age. This type of lifelong learning begins now—not after graduation from high school or college, but now. When a student employs the four drivers just listed, he or she will enjoy present academic success as well as success later in life. Academic success and lifetime success are not two separate entities, but rather form a continuum of achievements. This book is a guide for you as you continue your quest for current academic success—and, ultimately, lifetime success—for each of your students. It will strengthen your capacity to influence these teachable success drivers: attitude, effort, cognitive capacity, and focused strategy. Although we'll go into much greater detail in the upcoming chapters, let's give a quick overview to the big four here.

ATTITUDE

How often have teachers or parents said, "Don't give me that attitude." Words like these usually refer to a negative attitude. The student is seen as arrogant, demanding, ungrateful, lazy, selfish, or a host of other uncomplimentary adjectives. So how important are attitudes, and can they be changed? Attitudes matter! Attitudes are somewhat like moods, except they are more pervasive—with much greater intensity and duration. A mood can change quickly, but an attitude changes only through awareness and a true desire to choose a different one.

Attitudes influence and flavor a student's every thought and action. An attitude held on to tenaciously will have a significant impact on a student's life. In fact, one of the primary components of school burnout among students is a cynical attitude (Salmela-Aro & Tynkkynen, 2012, January 31). Academics can be tough, but nurturing a negative attitude toward school will only lead to complications, not solutions. For a student struggling academically, it is often easier to develop the "I don't care" attitude, which can be a camouflage for his or her lack of needed skills for succeeding in school. The negative attitude only perpetuates the problem. This is why a sagacious teacher will search for possible reasons for the negativity toward school and help the student discover solutions.

Seeing the relationship between negative attitudes and poor school performance brings us to the insight that students can get stuck in a vicious cycle. Many things in life may be out of a student's control, but he or she still has substantial choices. Attitude is one of the most important choices the student will make. This is the key—attitude is a choice. The real power lies within a student, not outside, in that his or her responses to life always determine the outcomes of that life. Students can never escape from themselves; their lives are always guided by their thoughts, actions, and attitudes—all of which are well within their control.

So where do student attitudes originate? One source is the family's attitudes in regard to school, academics, and behavior (Alonso-Tapia & Simon, 2012). Attitudes can be somewhat contagious and often begin in the home. Having little control over family life but enormous control over the classroom, teachers can focus on establishing positive attitudes within their classroom and school. Because many students are oblivious to having negative attitudes and have no idea how to change them, education becomes essential in effecting desirable change. Once a student learns more about a situation or groups of people, his or her attitudes can shift (Dell & Holmes, 2012). For example, once a student understands that a classmate stole his power bar simply because the other student is getting no lunch from home, his attitude might change about the incident. Teachers can assess dominant negative attitudes and determine a course of action to facilitate students' movement from negative attitudes to more positive ones.

Attitudes can and do change with learning and experience (Rodgers & Gilmour, 2011). Simply telling a student to change his or her attitude results in minimal change. Teaching, discussion, and modeling of a positive attitude constitute a great starting place. As students begin to comprehend that a positive attitude can often tip the scales in their favor, striving for a metamorphosis becomes vital and exciting for them. With a positive attitude being one of the major determinants of lifelong learning and success, it is certainly worth the effort to instill such an attitude in students. Students lacking a positive attitude tend to view all of life through a negative lens, which can undermine academics as well as respect of self and others.

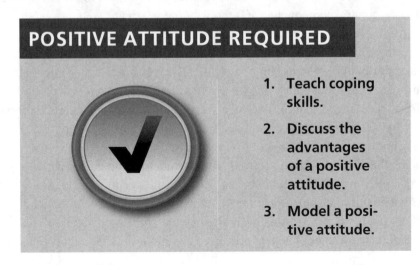

POSITIVE ATTITUDE REQUIRED

1. Teach coping skills.

2. Discuss the advantages of a positive attitude.

3. Model a positive attitude.

WHAT YOU CAN DO

- Teach coping skills for managing stress, which can sustain positivity in that kids are highly susceptible to stress and are very unlikely to have adequate coping skills.

- Establish an overwhelmingly positive classroom atmosphere so that no matter what's going on at home for your kids, your class is an emotional and social oasis.

- Model how you reframe life events and put them in perspective. Sharing your techniques permits students to see how you deal with the world and gain insights into self-regulation and optimism.

THE EFFORT PIECE IS VITAL

- **Persistent effort**

- **Focused effort**

- **Purposeful effort**

Persistence combined with focus and purpose maximizes effort.

EFFORT

All students, and especially struggling students, need to cultivate persistent, purposeful, focused effort to be lifelong learners. On the one hand, a student can rely too heavily on talent and natural abilities, resulting in little effort because he or she is already "good." On the other hand, some students refuse to try because they feel their situation is hopeless. Students tending toward either of these extremes have not grasped the simple fact that they can change where they are and where they are going through sustained effort.

In a classroom, it is the student who puts forth this sustained effort who will achieve. There are many variables affecting achievement, but the effort piece is always part of the puzzle (Miñano Perez, Castejón Costa, & Gilar Corbí, 2012). Effort is, of course, irrelevant if the task is not challenging. It takes little effort to have friends if one is outgoing and friendly. It takes little effort to achieve in classes that do not stretch the mind. It is the effort put forth under the hardship of doing that which seems unreachable, unachievable, and just too far out of one's comfort zone that produces substantial growth. Most students have no idea what they can achieve inside and outside the classroom, simply because they have never really tried. Afraid of failure, starting a challenging activity becomes a monumental task. Step one is movement. Take some action and start, turn off the nonstop doubting, and begin. Asking students to devote a set amount of time to an arduous task on a daily basis can get them moving, working.

Working with a real purpose can help the buds of success blossom into real achievement. Effort with a true purpose can result in significant gains in reaching the desired outcome (Pizzolato, Brown, & Kanny, 2011, Winter). A purpose can be as simple as a deadline, but even a deadline can become a true purpose for many students. Ultimately, an individual's true life purpose will be much loftier, more personal, and dream satisfying, but for now most students are in a state of transition when it comes to finding their true purpose. Help them out by offering lessons that hold relevance for them. Discover their world and apply what you learn from that world to your teaching. For example, in a science class, while studying plants, discuss some plants that are known to the students. Connecting their world to lesson objectives can provide many with the impetus for sustained effort.

Will there be setbacks or even failures? Yes! Missed shots, mistakes, even failures are all part of the bumps on the road to success. It is not the failure that is important—it is one's response and what has been learned that merit attention. In fact, the student who never experiences any failure or makes any mistakes is probably doing the bare minimum. Jumping into assignments, projects, and tasks with enthusiastic effort will result in some failures. A failure can be a good thing, especially when the student learns from the mistake, gets up, and keeps persevering with determination and focused effort. In advance of the upcoming Chapter Five on effort building, you can begin to build and develop effort in your students with these appetizers:

WHAT YOU CAN DO

- Reframe and redesign lessons to increase their relevance. Kids who are more invested in the learning do better. Find out what kids care about, then tie that into what you're doing.

- Show how setbacks are usually short term and beneficial. This will help students see that sustained effort will produce the desired results for them.

- Share a personal success you achieved through your sustained effort, such as getting a bachelor's or master's degree.

COGNITIVE CAPACITY

If one of your students is not a high performer, ask yourself, "Am I going to wish the student had more going for him (or her), but continue doing the same as before? Or am I going to learn how to build cognitive capacity and have the best school year of my life (simultaneously giving this kid a real shot at success)?" Some teachers label kids based on their alleged "smarts." Calling a student "smart" or "slow" might make sense if his or her cognitive capacity were fixed . . . but it's not. Yes, you can change the cognitive capacity of your students.

Cognitive capacity has only a small genetic influence—much of it is learned in school and at home. In a large meta-study on IQ by top cognitive scientists, the results were revealing: IQ is malleable (Buschkuehl & Jaeggi, 2010). For example, a group of sixty-five abused and neglected four- to six-year-old children with low socioeconomic status and an average IQ of seventy-seven were placed in adoptive homes. Eight years later, the children showed a documented *average gain* of fourteen IQ points, and some boosted their IQ by nearly twenty points (Duyme, Dumaret, & Tomkiewicz, 1999). In fact, school has a measurable impact on a student's IQ as well (Ceci & Williams, 1997). These home and school studies exemplify the immense impact of environment on IQ.

Researchers often use a tool called effect size as a measure of the potency of any newly introduced factor. Effect size is an accepted and standardized format used across similar studies to denote the strength of an effect on a particular outcome. Although an effect size can be negative (some factors, such as constantly changing schools, have an adverse effect on student achievement), the range of effect sizes is more typically from 0.0 up to 2.0. Small effects might be in the 0.20 to 0.40 range, whereas moderate to strong effects would be in the 0.40 to 0.80 range. Anything below 0.20 would have a minimal effect, and anything over 0.80 can have a dramatic effect on student achievement. Teaching thinking skills ranks a massive 0.69 in effect size, and teaching study skills sports a strong 0.59 ranking. These effect sizes are very impressive, given that an effect size above 0.4 is considered above average in educational research (Hattie, 2009). Students were trained using a format similar to playing a video game, which focused on working memory skills. This skill building actually boosted fluid IQ. In fact, the more hours of training students received, the greater the IQ effects (Jaeggi, Buschkuehl, Jonides, & Shah, 2011). This fluid IQ can be raised by purposeful practice *within nineteen days*. Kids are not stuck with the intelligence they have. There are, however, some teachers who are stuck in their thinking in regard to their students' intelligence due to their belief that intelligence is fixed. Building cognitive capacity means you have the knowledge, skill, and will to alter your students' ability to think—their processing speed, sequencing, attention, self-control, working memory, and vocabulary. You can't build their skills in these areas with occasional fun activities. You must discipline yourself to foster thinking skills with ten to sixty minutes of skill building per day, using existing content, over a period of one to three months.

We must not assume that students are limited to the skills and ''smarts'' they bring to school. We'll show you how to build cognitive capacity in Chapter Four, but for the moment, try these steps:

WHAT YOU CAN DO

- Begin to notice what gets students' attention in class and why. You'll need this information for the chapter on building cognitive capacity.

- Pay attention to *what* kids can hold in their head (working memory); *how much* they can hold (a word, a number, a formula, a sentence?); and for *how long* they hold things in their head. Can they hold the information long enough to manipulate symbols for math, science, or language arts? This background will serve you well when learning how to develop students' skills later in this book.

- Watch closely what happens when students are assigned work that involves processing information (reading, solving problems, writing a summary, and so on). Notice how they approach the task and how well they follow through. Processing skills are teachable, and we'll show you how later in this book.

FOCUSED STRATEGY

Strategies are necessary for maximum success. One of the areas of focus in this book is the application of strategies to setting, managing, and reaching goals. Truly internalizing the necessity of having a goal-reaching strategy or strategies is an enormous first step in becoming a lifelong learner. The real challenge for students is to determine which strategies are most effective to promote lifelong learning for them. Selecting a strategy is a very personal choice. Make no mistake: without a strategy or plan, students will never achieve to their fullest potential, and many will never comprehend how implementing success strategies could have made all the difference.

The simple truth is that for many students, contemplating the use of specific success strategies is not part of their mind-set. Some know that focused, hard work will benefit them, whereas others drift along, thinking and hoping some magic will happen to propel them to success. Focused, hard work is certainly a plus, yet the successful student needs even more. The strategic piece of the puzzle entails the student's executing specific success strategies to achieve a desired outcome.

Take the time to remind students of some fundamental success strategies for school. These can include such basics as having a dedicated work space, working with no distractions, budgeting time, completing homework, and coming to class prepared and on time. Before a student can advance to making more personal choices for success, he or she must already have taken the basic steps. A student with weak academic skills may never have mastered these fundamentals, or these strategies simply may not have worked. It is essential for students to begin recognizing what does and does not work for them.

As a teacher, you have a role that is similar to that of an emergency room physician. For each student, you must make a quick but thorough assessment of the situation and begin treatment. You may be thinking, ''They're in high school, they should already know how to implement basic school success strategies.'' The simple fact is that any needed skills that are lacking must be taught. Even university students can benefit from programs that teach them study skills and improved learning strategies. At Isfahan University of Medical Sciences, thirty-two medical students chose to participate in an optional course on learning and study skills. When compared to a control group of students who did not take the course, the students who participated in the course showed a marked improvement in time management, information processing, main ideas selection, and use of study aids (Haghani & Sadeghizadeh, 2011). This study demonstrates that even students in medical school benefitted from increased knowledge of effective implementation of success strategies. As unique as students and strategies can be, there are also some basic commonalities in each student's process of selecting and implementing success strategies:

1. The student acknowledges the need for success strategies.

2. The student evaluates old strategies, and selects new ones if needed.

3. The student implements the strategies for a sustained amount of time.

4. The student evaluates the effectiveness of the strategies.

5. The student makes adjustments as needed.

For a student to become a true lifelong learner, implementation of success strategies will always be crucial. If a student hasn't chosen strategies, he or she doesn't really have a plan for success. Beginning success strategies should be easy to implement. Consider, for example, the widespread use of pedometers as a strategy for increasing physical activity. Pedometers are affordable, accessible, and simple (Tudor-Locke & Lutes, 2009). Initial success strategies for students should be the same. A struggling student can be so overwhelmed by the complexity of a strategy that he or she totally forgets the desired outcome. You can start small and build from there. Remember the focus: first learn the application of strategies to setting, managing, and reaching goals.

When students have personal success strategies in place, they can handle with more finesse the unexpected events that are an integral part of life. With careful, continued implementation of well-selected strategies, students can begin their journey of lifelong learning and discovery no matter how tough their challenges may be. They will learn who they are, and will strive to remain true to themselves on their path to sustained academic and personal success.

You might argue that learning the right strategies is a by-product of life experience. We would support that theory, with one exception, and that is the amount of time spent in school. Teens only get thirty hours per week of life experience in school. This is why we need to make those few hours count. Let's review the primary drivers we've introduced so far.

The Four Lifelong Learning Drivers

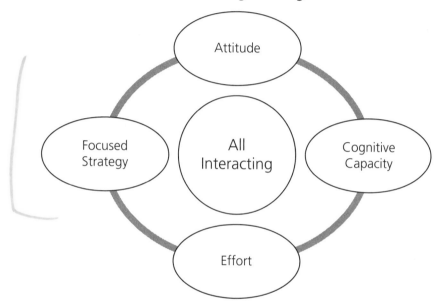

In each of this book's chapters, you'll get tools that will last for a lifetime. For now, consider the following:

WHAT YOU CAN DO

- Ask for and listen to your students' big dreams. If they don't have any, start introducing them (through biographies) to the big dreams of others.

- Encourage your students to set simple, short-term goals, and help kids learn how to develop monthly goals. In Chapter Eight, we'll show you how to assist them in managing these goals.

> • Ask questions of your kids about how they deal with obstacles. This will plant the seeds for later, when you'll help them arrive at a plan for selecting strategies. Students will need a working model for how to develop microstrategies and succeed.

TO SUM UP

For students to develop the lifelong learning habit, it is essential to help them focus on how they can enhance the four success drivers introduced in this chapter. Having a positive *attitude* is a core competency that's not usually part of any required curriculum. That it is not in the curriculum in no way lessens the importance of having such an attitude—in fact, without a positive attitude, a meaningful, productive life is doubtful. Having a status quo mind-set is really moving backward: students are either growing or shrinking, and it is almost impossible to remain the same. All of the drivers for success are teachable skills, and it is wise to take classroom time to assess and teach in these areas. Academics will improve!

Continued *effort* is a necessity for growth. Students should put in a genuine effort, giving 100 percent, not 99 percent. Yes, these numbers are high, but greater effort produces greater results. For students not exhibiting this effort, you, as their thoughtful teacher, can pause and seek reasons for their inadequate effort—and help them gain forward momentum.

Cognitive capacity, once falsely assumed to be fixed according to genetics, can be changed through teaching—and it can signify the difference between success and failure. Cognitive capacity should be strengthened, so take the time to learn how to use teaching to do this. It will change kids' lives.

The fourth driver, *focused strategy*, is woven throughout this book. Each chapter has been designed to increase your understanding of students and their brains, and the book points to specific competencies to augment learning. Each year, as you truly get to know your students, you will easily determine which kids need which strategies. As a dedicated professional, you will love the positive changes your see in your students when these strategies are implemented.

CHAPTER TWO

CHANGE YOUR STUDENTS' BRAINS

Many prior teachers referred to Carmen as a "piece of work." She appeared to be quite stubborn, used foul language, and refused most requests from adults. Someone without a background in counseling or psychology might have given her the armchair diagnosis of being "oppositional" and lacking social skills. Many of her teachers used the same tired stream of ineffective strategies: making requests, then demands, and finally threats. She bounced around from one detention to another, spending quite a bit of time in the counselor's or principal's office. The question on the table here is a simple one: Can Carmen change or not? Is she a lost cause, or is there hope for her? This chapter will show you not only that there is hope for her but also how to change her for the better.

A good deal of this book is dedicated to showing how change happens and what evidence shows leads to positive changes. This chapter will explore the following:

- The clear, peer-reviewed, high-end science demonstrating that your kids can change (at any age)

- The process through which the brain changes

- The real-world factors that you can use to foster change

Average teaching does not change brains—it's just babysitting. Kids could learn content from the Internet at home. But strong, high-quality teaching changes brains every day. We'll dig into how to become a high-quality teacher in the next chapter. But this chapter provides a crucial foundation. When there's no change in the brain of the student with whom you're working, there's no change in the student. And if you do not follow the brain's "rules" for change, you won't get the change you want. If what you're doing is not working with kids, notice that it is not working. Just because you're not succeeding, it doesn't mean what you're trying to do is impossible. Don't point fingers and blame the student. Find out what you don't know. Then roll up your sleeves and recommit to your will, your skill, and your capacity to help students grow and succeed.

CAN YOUR STUDENTS' BRAINS CHANGE?

Would you like a mind-boggler? Physical activity can make your students smarter. Voluntary gross motor physical activity (such as running) increases the production of brand new brain cells (Pereira et al., 2007), and this increased production is highly correlated with improved learning, mood, and memory. When we say the brain changes, we are not talking about a ten-minute change, such as increased blood flow or shifts in brain chemistry (those are powerful, but also temporary). Your students can produce new brain cells, leading to thousands of powerful new connections between cells and increases in cell size and even gene activation—meaning new behaviors, emotional responses, and cognitive processing can occur (Abel & Rissman, 2012).

Researchers are discovering that a whole range of seemingly nonacademic activities can help the brain grow and change. Playing challenging board games (such as chess) can increase reading (Margulies, 1991) and math (Cage & Smith, 2000) capabilities by improving attention, motivation, and processing and sequencing skills. Playing certain computer-aided instructional programs can increase attention and improve working memory in just several weeks (Klingberg et al., 2005), both of which are significant "upgrades" to the brain. Students are not stuck with a poor attention span. Instead of demanding more attention in class, you can train students in how to build it. For example, such websites as junglememory.com and www.lumosity.com have scientific, research-based brain-training activities.

The arts are also critical in helping brain development. Many arts can improve attentional and cognitive skills (Gazzaniga, 2008). As an example, arts can upgrade the mental system by teaching attention, sequencing, and processing skills. Students who struggle with auditory processing in their reading may find help from such brain-training sites as www.scilearn.com. To put it bluntly, building capacity to learn ("upgrading" the brain) *is much more important* than adding more content.

Among other reasons for helping students upgrade their brains, you get a greater return on your time as a teacher. If you fail to plan an upgrade for the skills your students need to absorb and process academic information, you are planning to fail. Students are not stuck the way they are. Brains can and do change, if you know how to facilitate this process.

What Drives Positive Changes in the Brain?

Experiences that are . . .

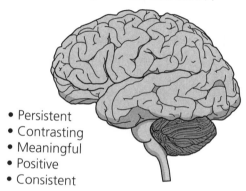

- Persistent
- Contrasting
- Meaningful
- Positive
- Consistent

Your life would stay the same if your brain stayed the same. But change does happen, and it is regulated by both genes and experiences. We also know that genes, once thought to be fixed, can be altered by multiple environmental factors. This phenomenon is called gene expression, and it allows humans to have a fresh, wide range of changes. For example, early life stress in infants can alter the expression of genes (activating a gene to express its primary function means "turning it on," whereas suppressing it means "turning it off"). In this case, early stress may activate genes that increase the risk of depression as the infant grows into adulthood (Gilman, Kawachi, Fitzmaurice, & Buka, 2003). So we have three sweeping factors that change the human brain:

- Genes (including gene actions, both inherited and programmed)

- Environmental factors (surgeries, play, interactions with family, injuries, accidents, exposure to toxins, scarcity or abundance of resources, and so on)

- Gene-environment interaction (known as gene expression, occurring when environmental factors—long-term nutrition variances, exposure to chronic or acute stress, learning, extended positive or negative social contact, and so on—affect our genes)

In other words, our subjective experiences, our behavior, and social dynamics can and do modulate gene expression and vice versa—a conclusion that would have been considered laughable a generation ago. For years, researchers thought the percentages were about equal: 50 percent genes and 50 percent environmental effects on who we become. Today, researchers believe the percentages are much more "muddled," and when we add up environmental effects and gene-environment effects, they total about 60 to 70 percent.

A core understanding is that the heritability of a trait (height, weight, and so on) is unrelated to its mutability. As an example, height is highly heritable (.85 to .90), but it is also mutable. In cases of neglect, an infant may have stunted growth. Alternatively, in South Korea, the average height of thirteen-year-old boys went up seven inches in forty years with better nutrition, a rate far too fast to attribute to genetics (Kim et al., 2008). What we see, over and over, is an interplay between genes and environment.

What Determines Destiny?

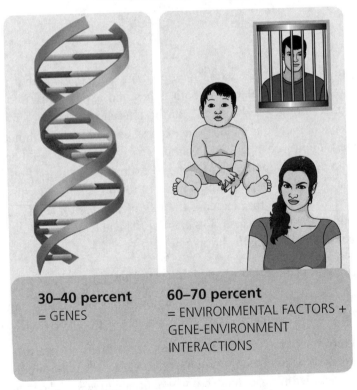

30–40 percent
= GENES

60–70 percent
= ENVIRONMENTAL FACTORS +
GENE-ENVIRONMENT
INTERACTIONS

Source: Adapted from Rutter, 2008.

As you can see from the illustration, genes alone contribute about 30 to 40 percent of how we turn out. Genes "code" for eye color, height, skin color, weight, hair color, and susceptibility to diseases. We know that environmental events can change us too. For example, if we get exposed to a disease (Lyme, herpes, polio, and so on) or experience head trauma, we will be different than if this exposure or trauma had not occurred. Events that are strictly environmental contribute about 30 percent to how we turn out. The remaining percentage (30 to 40 percent) is a complex interaction between the environment and our genes (Stoolmiller, 1998; Thompson et al., 2001; Turkheimer, 2000). In short, genes are not our destiny; they can either be expressed (turned on) or suppressed (turned off) in ways that will influence how we turn out. These environmental influences, including stress, nutrition, social contact, exercise, and academic skill building, can alter genes in newly discovered ways. They can also improve or impair attitude, health, social skills, and learning. When you influence your students, you are changing their brain in profound ways that may have a lasting impact. Before getting to the rules for how to change students' brains, let's define our terms.

We say brains can change. But what actually changes? Typically it is the quality and quantity of cells, cell connectivity, brain mass, blood flow, brain chemistry, and system reactivity. The term *malleability* broadly refers to the brain's capacity to change as a result of general, long-term experiences that affect it (for example, the brain might change with exposure to stress, repeated trauma, or even poor nutrition). Such changes tend to occur over a longer period of time, and with greater passivity than other types of change. Examples of malleability in action include

- Cells pruning as you age

- Gaining brain size

- Cells dying off

- Maturation of your brain

There is a different, more use-dependent type of change that we undergo. Whereas malleability is more general, neuroplasticity involves a specific type of change. The term *neuroplasticity* refers to use-dependent cortical reorganization. This process occurs when the brain changes in response to a specific, ongoing experience. When we learn to tie our shoes, ride a bike, speak a language, play a sport, build a boat, type, or play an instrument, the brain will change. Use-dependent cortical reorganization is a measurable and often significant remapping of the brain's topological real estate. In a way, it's like suburban sprawl: land once used for farming is sold, and now it is used for housing. If you lost the use of part of your brain due to a traumatic injury, in some cases a nearby healthy area could take over the functions of the affected area. This is a revolutionary concept; it says not just that the brain changes from experience but also that it alters its own allocation of tissue based on what you actually do on a daily basis. As a result, your three-pound brain is bustling with change. Examples of neuroplasticity in action include

- Learning a new language
- Building listening, thinking, or memory skills
- Trying out for a sport
- Learning to play an instrument
- Gaining problem-solving skills
- Making, building, or designing projects

Each of these items fits under the umbrella of "skill building." For your brain to develop its own customized processing capacity to meet your specific demands, certain conditions have to be in place. These usually are present when we learn new skills. But there are exceptions and specific guidelines that we'll get to in a moment.

CAN ADOLESCENTS CHANGE?

If you're wondering if there are exceptions to the change process among your students, there are none. If you've tried many things (approaches to discipline, strategies for motivation, incentives, and so on) before and have come up short, relax. There are long lists of others who are in a position similar to yours. The streamlined rules for accelerating changes in the brain were simply not followed; it's that simple. Some teachers did not have the "know how," and others did not follow through. Brains are designed to change; every brain changes, from genetic-based changes (such as maturation) and experience-based changes (such as from exercise). For example, simple maturation not only changes the brain but also is quite variable. Only about 30 percent of your students are likely to be at grade level: in any given school year (or student age), the majority of your students (approximately 70 percent) will be either more or less mature than the mean. This suggests that the rate of maturation varies quite dramatically.

In the classroom, some teachers have used "behavioral fracking" (increasing the pressure via threats, rewards, and punishments) to improve student performance, which has yielded little or no improvement. The conclusion by an unknowing or low-skilled teacher might be, "There's no hope." If you think that more pressure; more incentives; or more robust, intense consequences will get kids to behave or perform, you've got company; many others also feel that way. Yes, teens are going through some serious brain changes of their own, but additional change is possible. What's going on in the teen brain?

The changes from a sweet preteen to a teenager are dramatic. Teen brains resemble blueprints more than houses. Instead of thinking about a teenage mind as an empty house that needs furnishings, educators and parents would do better to understand it as the framing of a house that still needs walls, wiring, and a roof. Stop treating teenagers like adults; they're not. They have the highest car accident rate of any age group. They have the highest rates of depression, drug use, and suicide attempts (Dunlop & Romer, 2010). Teens are in a developmental fog and often make decisions even a nine-year-old would call stupid. They have sound biological reasons for the following patterns:

- **Susceptibility.** Given the same exposure as adults, teens are more susceptible to (likely to engage in) such behaviors as smoking, abusing drugs, and having unsafe sex. Teens are particularly susceptible to the risky extremes associated with novelty. Novelty juices up their unstable systems with brain chemicals like dopamine and noradrenaline. They choose short-lasting, immediate rewards over larger, delayed rewards. Their undeveloped frontal lobes play a significant role in allowing reckless behaviors. Students need intentional practice in assessing and managing their risk, and they need help finding "outlets" for taking risks (for example, sports, theater, community activism) that are safer.

- **Lack of planning.** Teens have trouble anticipating the consequences of their behavior because they rely on their immature frontal lobes to make decisions. They don't see options very clearly. They get confused easily under stress and rarely plan more than one move ahead. They're weak at risk management and have a tough time predicting the future. They can, however, be taught "if-then" thinking (for example, "If a driver is drunk, don't get in the car; call a taxi, always!") And they can improve their predictive skills by engaging in classroom scenarios that develop their ability to think about consequences and outcomes.

- **Emotional stewing.** Emotions are essential to learning, and teens are still learning how to understand and manage emotions. They are poor at reading emotions, and weak at selecting the right friends and getting their mind outside their own world of feelings. Through role playing and analysis of clips from movies and literature, students can learn to recognize and analyze expressions of feelings so that they better understand their own and appreciate those of others.

- **Crowd morality.** Teenagers will climb the moral ladder only as their frontal lobes develop. They spend a good number of hours every week using digital media (smartphones, laptops, texting, Internet browsing)—all unsupervised, most of it alone. To balance this, they often seek friendly (even if it's negative) peer clustering. But they're more likely to engage in risky behaviors when they are in groups than when they are alone, so it is essential that kids find positive social experiences, such as teacher-initiated groups including after-school clubs, hobbies, or sports.

- **Difficulty in self-regulation.** Teens face a wide range of neurochemical changes that they often struggle to manage. The changes can contribute to behavioral and personality challenges; increased anxiety or depression; tough-to-manage stress; eating issues (eating too much or too little, weight issues), and shifts in sleep habits. Teens are more vulnerable to all of these than adults are, and they have few coping skills. Although lecturing can often backfire, this means that it is still important to overtly teach self-regulation skills and show teens how to reframe issues, redirect attention, and de-stress. Teach these through example, role plays, and short podcasts, not lectures.

- **Substance abuse vulnerability.** Teens are extremely vulnerable to addiction, and compared to adults they are less cognizant of the effects of drug abuse—and their addictions are harder to break. They often see drugs as harmless, for the most part, and tend to believe that they can survive anything. Again, lecturing, especially giving the ''this is your brain on drugs'' talk, is ineffective. It is more effective to take a positive, brain-building approach by helping students see that they can be proactive in developing the ''brain they want.''

''NUDGES'' FOR CHANGING THE BRAIN

Does all this chaos and change suggest that the teen brain is too complex or ''messy'' for positive change? No, in fact, it's quite the opposite. The teen brain is *highly vulnerable to change*, and that's both a challenge and an opportunity. The brain's wild ride means that multiple systems and structures are undergoing massive changes—it's just not done maturing. In short, even if you have not succeeded so far, there is still hope. Maybe you'll need to change your approach. But first, it's time to finally learn how to change the brain. The following are powerful "nudges" in changing the brain:

1. Relationships—because they influence stress levels (lowering or raising them) and create a more "civil" teen through the development of a "give-and-take" reciprocity.

2. Attention and buy-in—because when the brain is alert and focused, and there's a strong behavioral relevance (for example, the potential for raised status, novelty, risk, and peer acceptance), the brain will change.

3. Mastery and autonomy—because developing mastery and autonomy supports the student's willpower, so that change is sustained for the long haul.

4. Brain health—because healthy brains make positive changes more easily.

5. Coherence and sense-making—because the learning has to make the task make sense, or there's no change. If a student feels confused, overwhelmed, or lost, the experiences will make no lasting changes in the brain.

6. Mistakes and error correction—because kids have to learn not just what is correct but also what is wrong. If a student learns the right answer (activating a particular connection), chances go up for getting that answer right at test time. But if the test also presents similar, equally plausible answers, the student may be confused. It is the error correction that tells the brain to suppress close but wrong answers. The process of making mistakes tells the brain what to enhance or suppress at the all-important test time.

7. Challenge—because this influences chemicals in the brain that tell us to try harder or relax. Too little or too much challenge and we quit learning. The perfect balance for learning is a slightly edgy, hungry-to-learn state with sufficient task challenge.

8. Time on task—because change is a physical process, and if we are to make those brain changes, we need enough time spent at a given learning task.

Brains rarely change through random life events. It does happen (for example, a car accident may lead to head trauma). But most of our changes come about via genes (we grow and mature, and our brain chemistry and hormones change) or environment (for example, marginal nutrition, a caring parent, or daily smog can all have an impact on how we change). The changes we are talking about making here are the kind that result from the practice of highly effective ''teachers.'' The ''brain-changing teacher'' could be a mentor, classroom teacher, coach on a school sports team, special education teacher, counselor, or music teacher. Not every effective teacher uses every single factor listed in the paragraphs that follow—but most of them use most of the factors to their advantage. The ones that are ''over the top'' successful may use nearly all of them, relentlessly.

Once you learn more about the brain nudges that will drive change in your struggling students, you may think, ''Oh, I knew that.'' The problem is that you're really saying, ''I've heard of that factor.'' But maybe you don't actually attend to that factor with rigor—or maybe you don't use it at all. In short, there are the big ideas (the brain nudges), and there is the reality, the integrity of implementation (the ''rules'' that you must follow to avoid getting only marginal results). Most teachers recognize reasonably good ideas, but the best teachers have the skill, will, and knowledge to follow the rules. In no particular order, here are the factors, along with the rules for implementation.

Brain Pusher One: Relationships (''Who Cares?'')

Teacher-student relationships can be a moderate to strong changer of student behaviors. Student-teacher relationships have a blockbusting 0.72 effect size in promoting student achievement (Hattie, 2011). You've heard the mantra: students don't care how much you know until they know how much you care. There are kids who may not need as much contact time with you as others. But in general, the kids who struggle tend to struggle for a reason. Most do need a strong adult role model. You may never know how important you are to the kids you work with, and they aren't likely to tell you. Most are not mature enough to come out and say it. Assume that relationships matter, and you'll be right more often than you're wrong. One more thing: remember how when you liked a teacher, you worked harder for him or her? That has not changed a bit.

WHAT YOU CAN DO

- Set aside time to learn about your students (beyond each one's name). Find out (gently and noninvasively) about what's going on at home. Be empathetic. Ask questions in a curious way—do not "interrogate." Share some of yourself to foster two-way rather than one-way conversation.

- Be unusually reliable. Kids who struggle may have had bad experiences (creating distrust) with other adults and are seeking hope and stability. If you mess up, be sure to apologize if at all needed and expect to get a great deal of "grief" from your students over inconsistencies.

- Remember that relationships are for the long haul. Your students may develop high expectations of you. For example, they may expect you to attend a function in which they are participating (a sporting event, a club event, graduation, a science fair, and so on).

Brain Pusher Two: Attention and Buy-In ("Selling" the Brain on Change)

Regardless of the process, goal, skill, or project that you want students to take on, you'll probably need to "sell" them on its value. Once you do, kids need to pay extra-focused, lockdown attention, because scattered attention won't change their brain. Your attention and focus give the brain all the information it needs to do error correction. The "buy-in" tells the brain, "This is important, pay attention, and save this!" (Polley, Steinberg, & Merzenich, 2006). As already suggested, if the brain's not buying in, the brain's not changing. We'll show you more on how to get buy-in and attention in Chapter Four on building cognitive capacity.

WHAT YOU CAN DO

- Establishing relevance is just one of the strategies to increase buy-in, which is where you come in. The goal is to connect constantly! Connect your students with yourself through metaphors, stories, and examples. You are the bridge from their learning to their personal lives. The teachers who have a powerful influence on their kids can make the connections, the associations, and the translations to render school learning relevant. Do not give up on a student; even if you and the student have a strong relationship, you may need to try out at least five to ten different strategies a month. What works one day may not work another day. Never let your teaching get stale.

- Provide an immediate success, so students see that you can deliver what you promise. Most students love it when you can demonstrate a memory system, such as the peg system, which attaches new content to already known "pegs," such as letters or numbers (for example, "One is the sun, and two is a shoe"); the use of acronyms; or word associations. Let them see instantly that they can learn and become more effective at their schoolwork.

- Buy-in often happens when you connect it in social ways (such as working with partners or in teams), making it more fun.

- Connect the content with what's happening in students' own lives, in their neighborhood, and among their friends. If appropriate, put students in small groups and have them come up with at least five connections between the task assigned and their own lives.

- Connect using mobile technology, innovative apps, and social media, because kids already believe in the value of these types of communication.

- Given students' developmental stage, it helps to make a strategy sound risky. ("First, here's the number for the fire department if we need to call them. I'm not sure if this experiment will work like it's supposed to. Want to try it anyway?")

- Ask students to break down their task into tiny components, so that they can feel very confident about their chances of quickly completing that task.

- Show what the finished "product" (for example, a student who has the skill) looks like to get them excited over completing a given task. Have a past student or high school graduate present to the class, or use YouTube clip tie-ins that will help make it all come together.

Brain Pusher Three: Mastery and Autonomy (Developing Ownership of the Change)

Mastery means that students can learn to appreciate the goal of developing expertise (versus doing what is "good enough" to pass a test). Autonomy means that students feel like they are "in charge" of their learning and are the primary variables to control their outcomes. Students are more likely to jump into a task that they can choose. Most kids like to be able to influence the content, the outcomes, the standards, and the process—and they prefer to regulate their effort. It is typically for teacher-initiated reasons that learning has low appeal to secondary kids (Norwich, 1999).

Mastery and autonomy are all about students' feeling like they are coming into their own, like they have some independence and capacity to "drive their own bus." Here, you give students ways to make the learning theirs. These two factors may also come about as a result of student choice or strong personal interest, or piqued curiosity, or matching with student values (such as being included or liked by peers) in the task. The research tells us that when you support (rather than battle over) student autonomy, helping students become more autonomous over the semester, you get better performance (Black & Deci, 2000).

WHAT YOU CAN DO

- Help students develop a checklist for the completed "deliverable." They can also create progress milestones to help them understand the kind of attention, effort, and persistence it takes for mastery. Help them learn to describe it, the attributes and qualities, so that they have a strong mental representation of mastery.

- Students do not need to have complete control over their learning. They only need to *feel like* they are in control. This is a critical rule: if we feel like we're in control, we're happier. This means that you as the teacher might preselect the possible choices for how to complete a given task, for example, and then let students "choose" which ones they want. Everybody wins.

- Autonomy does not mean that students must do everything alone. Use a 50:50 ratio when allocating class time: half for independent learning and half for social learning. Students need the experience of managing their own learning to strengthen that "in control" feeling. Students can feel in control even when they are working with others on a team.

- Provide support for students' autonomy. Give them the tools for learning (Internet options, partners, and control of deadlines, for example), and even help them design the evidence-gathering process, so they understand better each microstep for goal attainment. Then help them develop accountability, and give them feedback on their learning.

Brain Pusher Four: Brain Health

The brain health factor is a broad, catch-all domain that includes managing stress; avoiding head trauma (from skateboarding, driving, or snowboarding accidents, for example); eating properly; getting exercise; staying away from drugs; and managing emotional health. When your brain is healthy, it usually works well, and you also work well. When your brain has health problems, you usually have life problems. Each of these problems can be a powerful additive factor or adverse subtractive factor in changing the human brain. Some of the issues, such as head trauma (which often comes with accidents) and drugs, are common among those who struggle with risk assessment (especially teens, uneducated individuals, drug abusers, and the elderly). Others are those about which your students simply don't know much (controlling stress, eating right, and managing emotional health). Adult role models can play a significant part in this area because they often have the experience, perspective, and vested interest to strengthen healthier brain habits. Remind kids to take care of their brain!

WHAT YOU CAN DO

- Teach kids how to deal with their negative emotions. They need a group of simple "if-then" rules. For example, here's an "if-then" rule that you can teach them: *if* they feel put down or depressed about something, *then* they should ask just three questions: (1) "Am I a good person who usually has good intentions?" (2) "If I did do something wrong, what do I need to do to correct the wrong, and when can I do it?" and (3) "What do I need to do to forgive myself or think more positively about my future?"

- Avoid moralizing about lifestyle. Show them clear, high-quality images of what drugs do to harm the brain. Go online and get the poster called 'Which Brain Do You Want? (http://store.amenclinics.com/which-brain-do-you-want-poster-large). Show this to kids to help them see the damage drugs can do. Also teach students about how better nutrition can help them learn, feel more healthy, and have more positive days. Don't save this for a "health unit" at school. it is everyone's business on your staff to help kids be their best. One good teen health site is www.healthykids.nsw.gov.au/.

- Remind students that their biggest asset is their brain—and that the brain is very susceptible to injury; toxins (smog, smoke, and air with quality issues); and environmental adversity (lack of fitness, poor diet, and noisy, stressed living conditions). Tell them to put on their seatbelts, and to wear a helmet for every risky sport, including skateboarding.

- Teach kids better thinking skills with these seven "avoids":

  - Avoid generalizing with words like "always," "never," "everyone," or "every time."

  - Avoid becoming preoccupied with the negatives.

  - Avoid negative fortune telling, or predicting the worst possible outcome of an experience or situation.

- Avoid false mind reading, or believing you know what another person thinks, even though he or she has not told you.

- Avoid using words and phrases like "should," "must," "ought to," or "have to" that produce feelings of guilt.

- Avoid blaming others for the small, everyday problems in your life, such as disappointments, upsets, or changes of plan, and start accepting that you usually play a role in how your day turns out.

- Avoid thinking you have all the facts and answers; remain a curious learner forever.

Brain Pusher Five: Coherence and Sense-Making

Focus on ensuring that kids really do understand what's going on in a typical class (they may not want to admit they have no clue). Brains will change for the better when there is coherence and sense to the learning experience, and will change for the worse when there's chaos. In the classroom, unless kids understand *how* to read, *how* to summarize, and *how* to take notes, they'll be lost, without any sense of coherence. If the teaching is vague, some kids will feel too self-conscious to ask for help, and will simply go through the motions—and no brain changes will take place. In short, change comes with crystal clarity in regard to what is needed to acquire a skill or complete a process.

WHAT YOU CAN DO

- Stop asking kids if they have any questions about the content, skill, or process. It's too risky for them to admit they lack coherence or understanding ("My peers will think I'm slower than the rest of the class"). Start using simple feedback tools to ensure they really do understand. Ask them to write what they know so far, ask them to teach a neighbor while you eavesdrop, and continue to give feedback daily.

- Use metaphors and analogies. Learners already understand what a thermostat, strainer, toaster, surge protector, battery, or outdoor grill is. They understand (on a surface level) what an iPhone, skateboard, Mars rover, or garbage disposal is. Analogies and metaphors that incorporate simple household and backyard items help illuminate content (for example, "Your brain's hippocampus works a bit like a surge protector to limit the risk of overload").

- Always vary your teaching to include the use of illustrations, drawings, and graphic organizers. Ask kids to illustrate what they have learned, and check their work often for misunderstandings.

Brain Pusher Six: Mistakes and Error Correction

The brain is hardwired to learn from experience. In fact, you could argue that most of what you've really learned well in life came from the "school of hard knocks." It was the trial and error of living your life that gave you your wisdom, not a book. If you want students to get better at a skill or have an insight, they need to "have a stake in the game," and they must have opportunities to make, learn from, and correct mistakes. Why is the act of making mistakes so critical to changing the brain? Each of the systems in the brain that process our experiences is thought to be activated by our experiences of reward, feedback, and relevance (Kilgard & Merzenich, 1998). These everyday experiences are known to play a large role in producing changes in the brain. The mistake, followed by awareness and effort, will change the brain. This is why an active and thoughtful brain is better at realizing a mistake has been made, and even the subsequent reflection process can change the brain (Levy, 2007).

WHAT YOU CAN DO

- Make any feedback you give about the task, not the person. You damage your relationship with a student when you criticize or demean him or her.

- Be specific. What needs improvement, and what *exactly* can be done to make the needed change? For example, say, "Put the A/B function on the right side of the equation and see if that helps."

- Keep feedback real, and don't sugarcoat it. Give honest feedback in a kind, loving way. Otherwise, students can't possibly figure out what to do differently next time. Kids over the age of ten are better able to hear quality, constructive feedback than younger children.

- When possible, allow the task itself to provide feedback (for example, when you play the wrong note and it sounds bad, or when you play Simon Says and you're the only one standing). Making space for task-generated feedback means you'll make use of a successful (or failed) experiment, computer-based games that provide a score or ranking, or an object that students have built (such as a recorder, flute, or drum). This keeps the feedback fast and specific to the task at hand.

- In your feedback to students, focus only on actions over which students have control and that they have the power to change. This means concentrating on effort (doing more practice), strategy (for example, switching to a more effective study method), and attitude ("I will succeed" and "I know I'll make mistakes along the path to success").

- There are rare cases in which it's good not to reinforce a student's effort. When things go wrong, avoid praising effort. After an obvious failure, being complimented for "effort" not only makes kids feel stupid but also leaves them feeling like they are stuck and can't improve. When things go right, it's good to praise effort if that was a key factor in the success. It's smart to avoid praising ability. Otherwise students will think it was ability (rather than effort, attitude, or strategy) that made things work.

- Vary the feedback. Use notes, e-mails, visual cues, charts, rubrics, or checklists. You can also use peers, groups, teams, and partners to generate feedback.

Brain Pusher Seven: Challenge ("Games Worth Playing")

A fundamental concept to bear in mind when seeking to change any brain is contrast. If the brain continues to get the same experiences over and over, little change will occur. This is why teachers who ask students to keep doing a task that they fail at over and over will only create frustrated students. To get more dramatic change, you need to help students reflect and plan to make the experiences very different. This is also why a key factor is the degree of challenge inherent in the tasks completed successfully. In other words, it's got to be a "game worth playing." In sports, kids enjoy the game precisely because there is a game to it. The score is not predetermined, the opponent is not going to roll over and play dead.

What makes a task challenging? For one thing, the task must have a good "entry point." Notice the exact point where students are. Start skills just a touch lower than their grade or skill level. Ideally, they need to initiate the task where they can reasonably succeed and be excited to take it on. Now for the critical feature: you must be able to increase incrementally the difficulty and complexity of the task. With each success, this reinforcement builds confidence and boosts the "feel good" and, in addition, the "I can change" levels of dopamine. When dopamine levels are higher, we are more open to further feedback (Brown & Beninger, 2012; Tricomi & Fiez, 2012).

Increase skill demands by regulating time, support, and goals. Each time students do the task, let them back up a bit to review what they've already done. Then allow them to go as far forward as they can. One more thing: to make sure that the task is transferable from the specific situation it was designed for to a broader or simply different relevant application, you'll need to increase the range of the task and the complexity, as well as the task's variability and depth. As soon as the low-level task is mastered, start adding variations. Add more challenges, more people, stronger time deadlines, and more to hold in working memory. Then add other content and other contexts, such as a more pressure-packed test simulation.

WHAT YOU CAN DO

- Give learners an easy entry point with an opportunity to move up fast in task difficulty.

- Give students some control and choice over the task challenge. Just like in a video game, kids need to be able to go to the next level when they're ready, not when the teacher is ready. Make the task one continuous stream of increased challenges.

- After students have mastered the initial task, add broader and deeper challenges to ensure the transferability of the task. You can add more deadlines, higher standards, and a greater range of content, or introduce more complex circumstances with even fewer resources. For example, ask for the learning in a different application (at home, in other classes at school, or even at a job).

Brain Pusher Eight: Time on Task ("Time Is on Your Side")

The fact of the matter is, most of us really do like instant gratification. We want faster shipping on a product we order, we want our food to arrive quickly in a restaurant, and we want our students to learn fast and to improve their behavior even faster. But when it comes to learning, the brain does not work that way. Just about the only thing that changes our brain in an instant is trauma (and that's a terrible teaching tool)! To learn new skills, new behaviors, and new lifestyle habits, a student needs from four to twelve weeks (one to three months) for initiation, managing, coaching, encouraging, and feedback. Remember, the changes you're trying to effect in the student's brain require real physical changes. You're like an electrician trying to rewire a store for cooking that originally was used for yoga or selling hardware. It takes many new connections.

Although scientists have some pretty good ideas about how long the changes take, changing the brain is not yet an exact science. Why? There are countless variables, including (1) the existing state of the student's brain, (2) how diligent and relentless the change process is, (3) whether or not there is error correction to ensure mistakes are fixed fast, and (4) the strength of the student's motivation or buy-in. As a guideline, expect your change actions to be purposeful, intentional, and different, implemented for ten to sixty minutes a day, three to five days per week, for four to twelve weeks. Any reduction, weakening of focus, or pullback in this routine may compromise the results.

WHAT YOU CAN DO

- Use varying amounts of time for different tasks. The greater the number of neural connections involved and the more "rewiring" needed, the greater the time required. For example, learning a new vocabulary word can be done in minutes. But learning a language (music, math, or a new spoken language) will take many minutes per day (a minimum of 30 to 120 minutes) for at least three to five days a week—and it will take years to learn that language with confidence for the long haul.

- Set aside extra time for learning complex perceptual skills (auditory skills, reading skills, or visual processing skills), which is the second most difficult process (behind language learning) for the brain. Do not begin teaching these skills to students unless you're committed to the process over time. These skills will take many minutes per day (a minimum of thirty to ninety minutes), at least three to five days a week, for one to four months to be learned with efficacy and permanence.

- Begin with a simple, specific skill. Learning a narrow, single-dimensional skill (such as visual working memory for math, sequencing task components, processing for text summaries, delayed gratification for long-range goals, or self-control) is the third most difficult process (but it's comparatively easy) for the brain. This process will still take time. Set aside five to twenty minutes per day (a minimum of three to five days a week) for eight to twelve weeks so that students can learn the desired skill with lasting effectiveness and confidence.

- Create and manage students' expectations for learning. Frame the learning as a long-term process (if it's appropriate) from the beginning. Let students consider the time it takes for language learning, and what it takes for crops to grow, friendships to flourish, and skills to develop.

CARMEN REVISITED

You may recall Carmen from earlier in this chapter, who was thought of as a "piece of work." Well, it might be better to think of her as a "work in progress," which every one of us is. Some of us were dealt a pretty bad hand in terms of risk factors at home. Growing up is hard enough when you're in a stable home; for some, transitioning from child to young adult is challenging and often done without support, almost like navigating a minefield. Carmen came from a family in which her father left when she was two. Her mother had a series of boyfriends, none of whom provided any stability for Carmen. Her mother was working the late shift, and her hours (noon to eight o'clock at night) meant that she was unable to meet with teachers or see her daughter at home each night for dinner, connecting, or homework.

So what was it that got Carmen back on track? The first thing her school counselor did was start getting to know her better. Building a strong relationship is the starting point for any success with a troubled teen. Second, the counselor identified a small number of core life skills that Carmen needed ASAP. Because of the relationship that was built, Carmen bought into the process of building her strengths, her character, and her work ethic. The counselor provided more than just guidance—she presented options for life after high school, acted as a role model, and even made several home visits. Once Carmen saw how much others cared, she began to care. Carmen will not make the honor roll this year in school as a junior, but her grades are better. That's a good start. The question posed earlier in this chapter was a simple one: "Can Carmen change or not? Is she a lost cause, or is there hope for her?" You can see now that there is hope for her, and you've begun to learn how you can change struggling students like Carmen for the better.

TO SUM UP

This chapter laid a strong groundwork for changing brains. When you change a student's brain, you change the neural systems that help regulate decisions, behaviors, and feelings within a student. This is why we say that there are no students that we can, in good conscience, give up on. If what you're doing is not working, notice that it is not working. In Chapter One, we said that the general drivers of success are

1. Effort—you can influence this factor, and it matters a lot!

2. Focused strategy—if something's not working, change it.

3. Attitude—a healthy mind and body attitude can and must be taught and learned.

In this chapter, we focused on the specifics for rapid brain changing. Our new list includes the factors that change the school-age brain most:

1. Relationships

2. Attention and buy-in

3. Mastery and autonomy

4. Brain health

5. Coherence and sense-making

6. Mistakes and error correction

7. Challenge

8. Time on task

Each of these can be a huge driver in change. Reread the brain nudges and reread the ''rules'' for engaging these factors. Then roll up your sleeves, and recommit to your will, your skill, and your capacity to help students grow and succeed. We only ask that you don't waste your time with untested ideas and lack of follow-through. Life is short for your students. They need a daily ''pro'' (which is you) at changing their brain. There are no ''throwaway'' students—no students we can give up on. Follow these brain rules, and you can enjoy positive changes every day of the school year.

CHAPTER THREE

BEGIN WITH ATTITUDE BUILDING

Emily had done well in elementary school, with teachers often commenting about how smart she was. She loved the praise, but deep down wondered if she was really that smart. By the time Emily reached high school she had discovered that the best way to still appear smart was by not trying anything very challenging. This way she could avoid the failures that would make others think she was inadequate. She had bought into the idea that what others thought of her was more important than learning and growing. If something did not work out, it was easier to place the blame elsewhere than to admit to herself that maybe she wasn't all that smart after all. Emily was becoming quite unsettled about this whole issue of ''smarts.''

Then a savvy teacher introduced her to the winner's mind-set. She taught Emily that her brain and intelligence were not fixed, but rather quite malleable. Emily was told that she could learn how to learn more effectively and change her outcomes. While Emily was mulling over the teacher's ideas, a tough new writing assignment grabbed her interest. With some hesitation, she launched into the research. Caught up in the information, she began to write. The final product did not receive the A she had wanted, but she still felt elated at her efforts. She knew she had stretched herself in a way she had never done before. She had tackled a tough job and completed it. Her thinking was changing. She felt like she was taking charge of her mind, her feelings, and her life. She knew she was developing the winner's mind-set her teacher had talked about. Emily was feeling the deep self-fulfillment that comes from positive change and self-control.

THE GREAT ATTITUDE SECRET

The ''great'' secret is simple: attitudes are not stuck the way you see them. They can and should be changed and developed to optimize academic and life success. When you see kids roll their eyes at a suggestion you make, relax. When kids complain about things too much, hang in there. When you see kids who lack optimism, coping skills, or resilience, remember that their attitudes, like most others, are teachable (Seligman, 2011). If you don't like students' attitudes, don't get upset, frustrated, or angry. Roll up your sleeves and help facilitate a change in the attitudes that impair student progress. If you don't, who will? Attitudes, positive or negative, will have a tremendous influence on students' academic success, relationships, and satisfaction with life. Positive attitudes can ultimately alter the course of a student's life, for the better.

This chapter reveals the three most powerful attitudes for student success. Yes, there are many, many possible attitudes you could develop in young minds. But you don't have time to do a good job on everything. The three in this chapter will make a difference. Each will take a few minutes per week, but the rewards are tremendous. They will change how students think about themselves and their world, and will consequently have a positive impact on their success in school and life. These attitudes are critical for your students' success, and best of all, they are all teachable.

If you're wondering whether kids can just ''show up with a built-in attitude,'' it is possible. The genetic basis for attitude exists, but it is much less powerful than the experiential effect. How much less? In a large study on the genetic basis of optimism, additive genetic factors explained between 36 and 46 percent of the variation in optimism, mental health, and self-rated health, with the remaining 54 to 64 percent of the variation being due to nonshared environmental influences (Mosing, Zietsch, Shekar, Wright, & Martin, 2009). So, it's true, there is a genetic influence on our attitudes. The influence is not on what we think about, however, but rather on the strength of the brain's neurochemistry, which influences mood regulation. We know, for example, that dopamine influences our levels of optimism (Sharot, Guitart-Masip, Korn, Chowdhury, & Dolan, 2012), and that everyday actions and thought patterns can change these in your students. For example, the expectancy that there will be a pleasurable reward (such as a privilege, friendship, a raise in status, or a fun activity) will raise dopamine levels (Kurniawan, Guitart-Masip, & Dolan, 2011). These studies suggest that the ways kids feel and think are not fixed; influencing the brain through your actions is one of the ways that attitude can be modulated.

The winner's mind-set is made up of the following three attitudes:

1. Learned optimism

2. A growth mind-set

3. Personal accountability

LEARNED OPTIMISM

The phrase "learned optimism" was popularized by pioneering psychologist Martin Seligman. Notice that this phrase is in contrast to "genetic optimism." Seligman proposed that one can learn how to be optimistic through certain teachable processes, such as purposely cultivating productive self-talk. Optimism is the mental state of experiencing hopefulness and confidence about a potential future or outcome of something. It's not specific; it's a global tendency to believe that one will generally experience good rather than bad outcomes in life. This means that if a woman survives a car accident, she will feel grateful that she was not killed rather than angry that her life has been changed. Having the ability to live life with optimism as opposed to pessimism can yield amazing results. Moving students toward optimism is a very worthwhile goal to promote their success, as academic optimism can make a significant contribution to student achievement (Hoy, Tarter, & Hoy, 2006).

Students can learn how to handle their challenges, including academic challenges, by changing how they think about each situation. There's also a circular effect: optimism leads to a different way of thinking, and thinking through a tough situation, examining specific causes, and choosing how to react will lead to optimism. This process requires a form of self-talk, but not the simple repetition of meaningless phrases, such as "I'm the best student in the world." What is needed is a careful examination of the situation and how it could be handled differently, done without falling into the trap of negative generalities. Thinking about a situation analytically will lead to positive action. Without this type of thinking, a student will begin to feel a situation is hopeless and eventually give up.

Another way for your students to grow is for them to learn how to think about their own life experiences. Incident-specific and carefully chosen positive self-talk is powerful and can be employed across many settings for optimal performance. For example, positive self-talk is the most commonly used mental strategy in competition preparation for triathletes (Dolan, Houston, & Martin, 2011). Students can use this same mental strategy to pave their way to academic success. For some students, the continual increase in academic demands from parents, the school, or themselves often fosters pessimism rather than learned optimism. The solution is to develop in your students a specific self-talk strategy called the "IRC." Learning and implementing this success strategy can provide an essential tool for struggling students. Begin by teaching a basic formula $(I + R = C)$ that all students can use:

I is the incident, what has happened.

R is our reaction to the incident.

C is the consequences we experience as a result of our reaction.

The incident plus the student's reaction will equal the consequences. The simplicity of the formula can be misleading. You may be thinking, "Everyone knows that." Many students, however, still have not developed the skills to comprehend how their response to an incident can have a lasting impact. The "R" part is the true power piece: students cannot always have control over life's events, but they can develop control over their reactions. It is important to note that students will often react emotionally to many events before they move into a rational response. The stress of the incident (most memorable ones are stressful) will trigger stress hormones, having an impact on brain structures involved in cognition (Lupien, McEwen, Gunnar, & Heim, 2009). Students must have time to calm down before considering an appropriate reaction.

Explain the formula to students using a common event that most of them have probably encountered, such receiving as a low grade on a test. Getting the low grade becomes the incident. At first, many students will simply react rather than choosing their response. Discuss with the students possible self-talk choices, making sure they are calm first. Provide examples of optimistic self-talk. Their thoughts will have a great impact on their feelings and behavior. By choosing their self-talk, they are deciding the ultimate outcome of any given situation. Training the mind to use positive self-talk is comparable to training the physical body—both take time and effort. We call this portion of the mental training process the law of positive consequences.

POSITIVE VERSUS NEGATIVE CONSEQUENCES

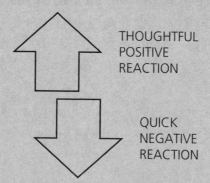

THOUGHTFUL
POSITIVE
REACTION

QUICK
NEGATIVE
REACTION

The well-selected, thoughtful response always results in more positive consequences.

WHAT YOU CAN DO

- Teach reframing skills. ("Yes, that was very annoying. But life goes on. Now, how can we turn this experience into a positive, useful lesson for next time?")

- Teach redirecting skills. ("Now that was *no* fun! How about if we shift gears and take a quick energizer break?")

- Teach the skills of wearing another person's hat. ("Wow, that was some terrible wind damage. Good thing there are plenty of contractors in the area who are looking for work. That'll be a source of good jobs for a lot of workers for quite a while.")

- Model and teach optimistic student self-talk:

- "Okay, I didn't pass that one, but I'll pass the next one."
- "One bad test grade won't kill me; I'm really a good math student."
- "I can easily schedule more study time."
- "There are lots of things to try, like eating a good breakfast."
- "Having a study buddy seems to help me; I'll go back to that."

Notice that the preceding responses are not excuses, and the student is not putting himself or herself down. When students start saying, "I'm stupid," or "What's the use?" they may be exhibiting a fixed mind-set, whereby students believe they cannot change their thinking. The winner's mind-set is the total opposite—the student takes the adversity in stride and moves on. The self-talk becomes an internal positive script. The same technique can be used for any situation with negative potential that a student routinely faces. For example, consider a student with a sibling who constantly uses a favorite put-down. Knowing the put-down is coming, the student can use preplanned positive self-talk to avoid reacting in a negative way. It is a way of actually disputing the statements internally, which is imperative. Using selected positive self-talk will help kill the negative thoughts.

Anything that we do over and over is likely to become a habit. Students' repeated ways of thinking can be habit forming and greatly influence their beliefs in regard to their ability to do well in school. Students' belief in their own ability to regulate their learning and academic achievement will contribute to obtaining scholastic success (Bandura, Barbaranelli, Caprara, & Pastorelli, 1996). Students need your instruction and encouragement in this essential skill. It cannot be left to chance. A great starting place is to become aware of negative self-talk in students by identifying patterns of continual negativity in their writing or conversations. Seek informal opportunities to discuss their negative patterns, while always respecting their confidentiality.

In the classroom, role plays could be used to demonstrate the I + R = C formula. If you use examples of incidents that are relevant to the students and are creatively interesting in your setting, students will begin to comprehend the power of their choices. You may have some students who have never realized the plethora of available responses to a specific incident. Habituated responses are well ingrained, and it takes awareness and focused effort to change. Your willingness to model positive self-talk in the classroom, coupled with persistent reminders to reduce negativity, will produce a classroom with increased optimism. Demands on teachers can be endless, and you'll need to make every minute count in your classroom. Teaching positive self-talk with occasional review will reduce your time expenditure in the long run, and will result in students who are more optimistic and hence put out better effort and sometimes simply will not give up. That is priceless.

A GROWTH MIND-SET

One of the many assumptions about success is that superior intelligence or talent is the key to unlocking it. In addition, there is the assumption that the talent or intelligence is fixed and cannot be changed. Countless students, parents, and teachers buy into this ''fixed intelligence'' myth. This false belief has many tenets to it, including that all of intelligence is inherited, and that the inherited intelligence is the primary contributor to a student's grades. Have you ever thought, ''The apple doesn't fall far from the tree''? It's not uncommon at a parent-teacher conference to hear a parent say, ''I was never very good at math either.'' But is it true that the student cannot really change or get better? Are students stuck where they are? The good news is no, they are not.

What we believe about the human brain today is radically different from what the prevailing beliefs were just a generation ago. The new thinking is that we can change our brains, and our brains change every day. In a study with middle school students, half were the control group and had no intervention. Students in the other group, the experimental group, were taught that intelligence is malleable and that their brains could grow and change. That was the only change made. The students in the control group displayed a struggling downward trajectory in grades, which commonly happens in middle school. But students in the experimental group, who believed they could change, actually improved and did much better than the control group over the following two years. In short, one change, one improved attitude, and students achieved more (Blackwell, Trzesniewski, & Dweck, 2007).

A similar study supported the view that just introducing the growth mind-set theories (using biased short articles for students to read) can influence patterns of information- and experience-seeking. This is powerful evidence showing what a difference targeted teaching can make. Student attitudes were affected by the teacher's purposeful behavior in regard to attitude shaping, and the students improved academically (Mangels, Butterfield, Lamb, Good, & Dweck, 2006). On the surface, it seems like such a small intervention, and it is. But many actions and behaviors follow a new thought.

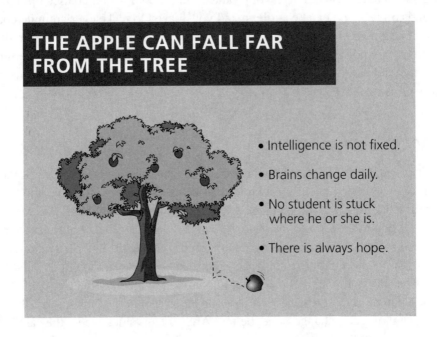

THE APPLE CAN FALL FAR FROM THE TREE

- Intelligence is not fixed.
- Brains change daily.
- No student is stuck where he or she is.
- There is always hope.

For many students, entering middle school begins an academic demise. They, too, buy into the fixed intelligence myth. This, coupled with the reality of changing bodies, surging hormones, brains that are undergoing reorganization, and increased academic demands, starts what could be called the "great separation." Some students move ahead, while others begin falling behind. All are experiencing the physical changes and the increased academic demands, so why do some make it while others do not? The key is not students' intelligence or talent; it is their attitude about effort and their determination to be successful. It is the belief that their effort is as important as—or more important than—their intelligence quotient. This willingness to put forth continual, purposeful effort is known as the growth mind-set.

There is a rare power in focused, ongoing effort. Each new grade level for a student can initiate a change for the better or for the worse as a response to the increased academic challenges. For some, there's a helpless, unresponsive pattern characterized by a lack of persistence (DaFonseca, Cury, Bailly, & Rufo, 2004).

For some students it will be middle school, for some high school, and for others college or graduate school—each student will eventually face that invisible wall that says, ''You have reached your limit, this is too hard.'' At that moment of new challenge, the student's life direction could go either way. So why don't all students just buckle down and work harder? Some are limited by a common belief that they are stuck with their brain the way it is, the belief that their brain can't change. They bought or were slowly indoctrinated into the big lie that says our intelligence is fixed and effort will only get you so far. How easy is it for students to cast aside this thinking and believe that their planned, focused, long-term effort will have positive results? It's not easy at all; in fact, it's very hard.

Among the biggest culprits in perpetuating the fixed mind-set are classmates, teachers, and parents who have told these kids all their lives how their brain is fixed. Certain students have done well in school, and test scores verify it for them. They may have gotten by for years with very little hard work. They enjoy feeling that they are intelligent, and when they hit that invisible wall, it's a real shock. They soon realize that this work is hard and may start thinking it's beyond their ability. Not knowing what to do, and certainly not wanting to let anyone down, they quit trying anything too challenging. They know they can still be their old, successful selves if they stick to the easier work. They pretend they don't care, or ''I could do it if I really wanted to'' becomes their mantra. We start hearing things like, ''I wasn't getting anything out of the class,'' or ''It was just too boring.'' These students have adopted a fixed mind-set rather than a winner's mind-set.

As educators, we must be cognizant of the overuse of such labels as ''smart'' and ''intelligent'' in the educational community. Labels are used in meetings, in conferences, and essentially anyplace students are discussed. Intentions are good, but outcomes can be very limiting for students. As you become aware of the overuse of labels, reflecting on the following could bring about a different mind-set for you—which you can then use to effect change in the mind-sets of students and parents.

WHAT YOU CAN DO

- Teach kids about the brain. Tell them that the brain can change, and that IQ is not fixed. Remind them of this often.

- Avoid labels. Drop the use of such words as "smart" and "intelligent," as well as their opposites. Instead discuss progress in terms of benchmarks. ("Here's where you are now. Here's where we want you to be by next week. What do you see we need to do next?")

- Say to students, "Before you began, you thought you could succeed. I love that optimistic, positive attitude. It was that powerful attitude that kept you going and helped you succeed." (attitude affirmed)

- Tell students in advance, "We will *all* experience failures now and then. I don't mind if you fail; it's what you and I do *after the failure* that determines our success. Do you get up off the floor after the failure, learn from your mistakes, and charge ahead? That's what will make you successful." (attitude affirmed)

- To foster perseverance, give students specific feedback and praise them for effort rather than for only the final product. By praising or grading effort, you are not saying that poor work is okay. Instead you are helping learners focus on the fact that continued hard work will reap untold benefits for them.

As you use selective, specific praise with students, teach them to use it also. For example, on major assignments, have students both rate their effort on a scale of one to ten and write a positive comment about the work. Students will soon discover the correlation between effort, hard work, and success. If you have ever struggled to reach a personal or professional milestone, consider sharing this with the students. Your honesty will enrich your relationships with your students and help them internalize the notion that everyone has to persevere to reach personal success. We like to call this specific process of growth positive self-talk.

Developing Positive Self-Talk

Fixed Mind-Set	Winner's Mind-Set
I have no sports ability.	Practice is making me better.
I'm not very intelligent.	By studying, I can improve.
I just can't draw.	I'm learning to draw by following the book's steps.
I'm not a math person.	A change in attitude, strategy, or effort can improve my math skills.
Picking an easy project makes me look smart.	This project will be hard, but I will learn a lot.
My school says I'm gifted. I can't afford for the work to be too hard for me.	Even though I'm gifted, I still have to work hard at challenging tasks.

PERSONAL ACCOUNTABILITY

The final of the three attitudes is key to building a feeling of ownership and responsibility in regard to one's own success. This attitude is personal accountability—a sense of responsibility that a student feels good about and even embraces personally. This ''accountability attitude'' means that, when appropriate, we understand that we must hold ourselves accountable for what we think, how we feel, and the actions we take. There is a growing emphasis on accountability in the educational community, often leading to raised stress among almost all the primary stakeholders. There is also a trickle-down effect as the new demands of accountability in our school systems lead to teacher stress. And when teachers are stressed, kids feel it too. Often students are at the bottom of this accountability waterfall, as some ''above'' them seem to ''pass on'' the stress to others.

In the classroom, we hear students muttering the classic statements, ''She said it first,'' ''I forgot we had homework,'' ''Everyone else is doing it.'' Being personally accountable does not magically happen to students. Many students have had no other model in life besides one of blaming others. In fact, some have nearly become experts at the ''blame game.'' By blaming someone or something besides himself or herself, the student feels he or she is no longer accountable or responsible. The blame game rears its ugly head as parents blame teachers and teachers blame parents for the behavior of students who will not hold themselves accountable for their work and actions—a cycle that only reinforces students in their avoidance of assuming responsibility.

Why is personal accountability so important? The process of choosing to claim responsibility for the actions you take is powerful because it reminds you of the effects you have on the world and your ability to make choices. You feel less like a victim and more in control of your life when you can say, ''I chose to act that way.'' Again, this is powerful. Personal power for students represents their willingness to take responsibility for the choices they make. Their lives will always reflect their choices back to them. When they pretend that nearly everything that goes wrong is someone else's fault, they are saying they have no power over their lives. When they take responsibility for their choices, others know they can count on them and even trust them. This newfound power can be exhilarating for students. A feeling of accomplishment results from accepting the risk of being associated with their own actions in the public eye and seeing the process, even when there may be initial discomfort (Bernard, Mills, Swenson, & Walsh, 2005). Here are some ways you can help students identify their own effects and, over time, develop their own personal accountability.

WHAT YOU CAN DO

- Point out to students with role modeling, Socratic questioning, and positive inquiry all of the moments at which they made choices so they know that they are far more in control than they think they are.

- Accept no excuses (except in rare, unpredictable circumstances). Students need to know where they do and don't have control so that they can embrace accountability when appropriate.

- Exercise patience while maintaining high standards for all. Learning to "think this way" (embracing accountability) is a learned skill; it's not genetic. Don't just tell kids about it. Walk them through the mental habits again and again.

- Use a brief session of classroom time to help students identify the moments, situations, and decisions in which they choose how things turn out (such as getting to class on time or turning in an assignment on time). Reinforce this repeatedly over a semester so that it becomes a mental habit.

Accountability Within Relationships

This notion of personal accountability can be quite confusing and even overwhelming to students. For example, is everything that happens to a student his or her fault? That notion would scare kids away from the process of taking responsibility. And how does this accountability play into the relationships each student has? Here we explore the role of accountability within a relationship. Why? We live in a world with others, and most students consider their relationships important.

Students make agreements and promises every day. For example, "Hey, let's meet in the cafeteria at 12:15 at the usual spot. See you then." If a student breaks his or her word, there's a process that can help maintain personal accountability and keep the relationship positive. The three steps are

1. Acknowledge the part you played in the broken agreement. ("This was on me. I did not plan my day well and was late. It was my mistake.")

2. Apologize without strings. This means you tell the other person that you know you made a mistake, and you apologize for broken trust, the waste of that person's time, and the frustration he or she may have felt. ("Listen. I am really sorry. I know we were supposed to get together at 12:15, and I wasn't there. No excuses. I hope I didn't mess up your whole lunch hour.")

3. Make amends. ("I feel bad about standing you up. You're a good friend, and I owe you one. How about if I help you with that math class you were struggling with yesterday? I'm pretty good at math.")

In other words, teach kids the right way to navigate through their day, with personal responsibility. To begin to restore trust with someone they have mistreated, they should start with going to the person who was affected, apologizing, and making a new agreement or plan of action. If talking in person is not an option, a student could call, text, or send an e-mail. A simple "I'm sorry" can at least start to mend many relationships. Making excuses, such as "I couldn't help it," is usually counterproductive. Students will need your patience as they develop their ability to create, maintain, or restore trust. Being trustworthy and apologizing when trust is broken are practices that build personal accountability and often take weeks or months to learn.

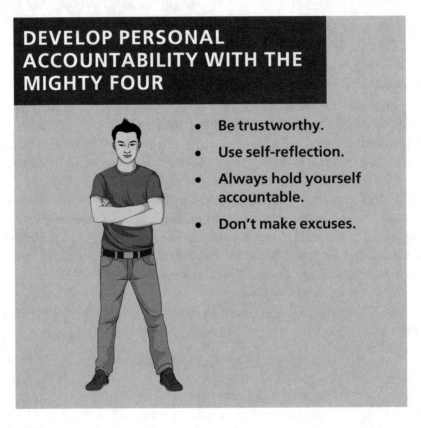

DEVELOP PERSONAL ACCOUNTABILITY WITH THE MIGHTY FOUR

- Be trustworthy.
- Use self-reflection.
- Always hold yourself accountable.
- Don't make excuses.

Shape the conversations with your students about personal accountability with the thoughtful exercising of power. Give kids more responsibility in increments and refer to it as "power with accountability." As an example, they can play music in the classroom or manage the movement and activity levels by leading energizers. Students love having power over their lives. What to wear, the state of their room, their choice of friends, how they spend their time, and what to eat are all areas in which students exert their power. Students who are enjoying power in some areas often want to extend that power to all areas, especially academics. Self-reflection plays a critical role in this self-regulation (Lyons & Zelazo, 2011). As their teacher, you will be able to watch as students begin to be the true masters of their lives. Help them along the road by never accepting excuses from them, and be willing to recognize the difference between excuses and those rare situations that are truly out of students' control.

When students start taking ownership of what they do and say, and stop blaming others for the situations that occur in their lives, they are developing their sense of power. They certainly cannot control everything that happens in their lives, but they can start controlling how they respond to what happens. As an educator, you have the opportunity to facilitate this aspect of the winner's mind-set in your students. The ultimate power is present when they can say, "I am accountable for how I respond and what I do."

In our fast-paced, constantly changing, high-tech society, students need your guidance more than ever. Much of the technology available to students, such as cell phones, has opened the door to a new world of issues. For example, text messaging is removing the consequences of awkward in-person interactions, leading to a reduction in the ability to communicate in face-to-face social settings (LaBode, 2011). When a student can simply respond to a broken agreement with "My bad" and ignore the rest of the other person's feelings, relationships can get damaged quickly. Show kids how to text responsibly if you teach in the language arts.

To *always* be a role model, which you are, is a daunting task. Keep using the word "power" whenever possible. Students have heard the words "be responsible"—and seen signs saying the same thing—ever since they started school. The words have lost their punch. To be powerful is much more appealing to students. Yes, responsibility may sum it up for you, but not for most students. Be willing to use new terminology to achieve the desired outcome. Teaching your students to do what needs to be done, when it needs to be done, and following this philosophy ourselves, is a powerful thing. Here are ways to foster the mental habit of accountability and responsibility.

WHAT YOU CAN DO

- Teach students how to text in ways that strengthen accountability. ("Here's the plan: I'll do this, you'll do that . . . "). Show them how to make amends ("So, so sorry. I blew it. You are important. Can I make this up?")

- Set crystal clear expectations about what is excellent and what is the right thing to do.

- Model the right behaviors with students, even sharing with them tough decisions you had to make in your own life and why you chose what you chose. Be sure to embrace responsibility as a positive form of power; don't make it "heavy" or a burden.

- Be consistent with students so they can trust your values. Increase students' control over their classroom life at the rate at which you increase their responsibility. You can't "make" a student responsible when he or she has no control over the situation.

- Reinforce learners' choices. Give them kudos for showing accountability so they know that you are noticing.

TO SUM UP

The chapter opened with the story of Emily, a student who was struggling. As she was exposed to attitude shifts, her world slowly began to change. She saw her attitude as simply her way of running her brain. This is a critical "ah-ha" for students: attitude is not something that exists by random assignment. It is shaped every day by the habits of thinking. Change your mental habits, and the attitude changes. As the attitude improves, so will your daily decisions and results. This chapter has shown you that attitudes are teachable.

As you set your sights on success for your students and for yourself as an educator, remember that a winner's mind-set will trump an attitude of fixed (or stuck) smarts every time. This is great news for you. Without this knowledge, it would be so easy to stop putting in the serious effort that characterizes what you do on a daily basis. Yes, you have worked with a struggling student and questioned if your efforts really made a difference. What you do does make a difference. What your students do does make a difference. No one is stuck where he or she is.

It is liberating to know that each individual possesses enormous power over his or her life. Yes, things will happen. You will get caught up in circumstances beyond your control. Yet as you support students with wiser choices, you can feel victorious. And you know that if students are willing to put in the extra effort, change their self-talk, and embrace accountability for their daily actions, they will have developed a winner's mind-set.

As you know, this chapter has focused on what you can do for your students. Undoubtedly, you've noticed that it's hard to teach others something that you don't know well yourself. Let students in on your secret: you are also developing your own mind-set. Begin by developing the winner's mind-set in yourself, for it is only then that you can teach it to students. Use your positive self-talk when the inevitable setbacks come. Assume the responsibility of ''running'' your own brain. By doing this you are giving yourself the power of choice. It will be your choices, your actions, that determine the successes you experience personally and professionally.

Student Handout: Manage Your Own Brain

- **Monitor your "self-talk."** *Self-talk is the internal conversation you have with yourself. Sometimes you talk to yourself with negative self-talk, saying things like, "This is too hard for me," or "I'm not good at this." Other times you talk to yourself with positive self-talk, like "This homework is interesting," or "I can do this even though it's hard." Once you learn to recognize self-talk, you can stop the negative dialogue and turn it into a positive one.*

- **Don't buy into the "labels."** *School is a place where it is easy to feel labeled. "Bad at math." "Popular." "Fabulous artist." Even when labels are positive, they can lead you to make assumptions about yourself and others that may not be true. Remember: there is more to you than any label can describe.*

- **When you do get a bad grade, respond with increased effort**. *Let's face it, bad grades can be discouraging, but there is a better response than letting them get you down, and it is very simple: work on working harder. Maintain a positive attitude, and ask for help when you receive a negative evaluation. This process will eventually become second nature to you.*

- **Keep your word, so others will trust you**. *If you are known to be trustworthy by your teachers and fellow students, they will have confidence in you and be even more willing to help you. Teachers will believe you if you get in a situation where you have to say something like "The dog ate my homework."*

- **Learn to be an actor, not a reactor**. *Part of never giving up on yourself is training yourself to act when bad outcomes occur . . . because they will occur. Investigate what happened, and don't go into a shell. Don't blame others or blame yourself; train yourself to analyze bad outcomes and come up with a solution for the next time, instead of going into negative reaction mode.*

CHAPTER FOUR

BUILD COGNITIVE CAPACITY

Marcus seemed to want to do well, but something always got in his way. If it wasn't one thing, it was another. He would act a bit scattered at times, then he'd get back on track for a short while. He struggled with getting organized and would lose his papers and homework. He would start a project too late to get it done. Often forgetful, Marcus never really stopped to reflect on his results and see the pattern he had created. He just could not predict the outcomes of his activities, and he would stay on the same track even when it was leading nowhere.

This chapter is about building capacity in students. Here we refer to the capacity to think, organize, and learn successfully. Many teachers talk about a student's "talent," or they say, "She's got it," as if certain students possess some mysterious "mojo." The fact is, most of what we call student capacity is a cluster of skills known as "executive function." This chapter will show you that (1) these skills are the critical drivers of student learning; (2) they are teachable; and (3) the "learn to learn" strategies are easy to learn, teach, and use as long as you're committed to your students' success.

CAN YOU IDENTIFY THE REAL ISSUE?

You may recognize, in the preceding passage, the challenges Marcus was having. They all related to poor executive function. For a student to do well in school, his or her brain must be relatively healthy. It does not need to be perfect. Everyone has a fault-tolerant brain, which is good at compensating and doing "work-arounds." Having such a brain means that you can succeed at a task even if you have to find an unconventional approach to get it done. Together we could dream up a list of specific skills that students need to have to make it in school, but it's already been done—the aggregate is called executive function. Among the many possible parts, we've chosen to explore these "big five":

1. **Self-control**: the capacity to restrain impulsivity

2. **Processing skills**: auditory, visual, and tactile

3. **Attentional skills**: the ability to engage, focus, and disengage as needed

4. **Memory capacity**: short-term and working memory

5. **Sequencing skills**: knowing the order of steps in a process

Your students do not need to be superior in all of these to get good grades. However, they do need enough of each, as well as compensatory strategies to fill in any gaps, if they are to succeed. The good news is that students are not stuck the way they are. Their success is dependent on a set of executive function skills, which are malleable and trainable, and can be taught and upgraded by educators like you. If you don't do it, who will?

It is admirable to raise standards and have high expectations. But it is not enough to wish and hope that something dramatic will happen. To make progress happen for each student, you've got to enable and build his or her brain's executive function. When you teach content, remember it takes learning skills to learn it. If you simply try to cram more content into the same brain, without enhancing the executive function capacity, the student will get overwhelmed, bored, and frustrated, and failure will be likely. The good news is that learners can achieve success, and that strong teachers can lead them to it. Executive function is the critical toolbox for student success.

COGNITIVE CAPACITY BUILDING BEGINS WITH EXECUTIVE FUNCTION

The research literature highlights the key role of executive function skills in cognitive capacity building for school success (Molfese et al., 2010). Weak executive function has been at least partially implicated as a factor in deficits in reading comprehension (Cutting, Matarek, Cole, Levine, & Mahone, 2009); math skills

(Lan, Legare, Ponitz, Li, & Morrison, 2011); emotional development (Rhoades, Warren, Domitrovich, & Greenberg, 2011); vocabulary (Stevens, Fanning, Coch, Sanders, & Neville, 2008); sociability (Checa, Rodríguez-Bailón, & Rueda, 2008); and many other academic necessities.

The research also suggests that executive function deficits can mimic the effects of attention deficit/hyperactivity disorder (Willcutt, Doyle, Nigg, Faraone, & Pennington, 2005); auditory processing disorder (Chermak, Tucker, & Seikel, 2002); fetal alcohol syndrome (Don, Mateer, Streissguth, & Kerns, 1997); preterm birth (Mulder, Pitchford, Hagger, & Marlow, 2009); brain injury (Kim, Whyte, Hart, Vaccaro, Polansky, & Coslett, 2005); and poverty (Waber, Gerber, Turcios, Wagner, & Forbes, 2006), among others. All of these have been shown to have an impact on academic performance and future life success.

Struggles with executive function may also give rise to secondary challenges, such as performance anxiety or a sense of overload, which can further sustain executive dysfunction (Denckla, 2007). This cycle may place students in danger of being labeled by adults as ''lazy'' or ''irresponsible,'' rather than the adults constructively addressing students' underlying needs (Denckla). However, teaching children strategies for overcoming executive function challenges often opens new doorways leading to achievement—and to new future directions. So what have we learned about executive function so far?

1. It is not just one thing; it's a cluster of skills.

2. It is very powerful.

3. Many symptoms of executive function deficits in struggling students mimic problems associated with other issues.

We now turn to each of the big five executive function skills, beginning with self-control.

THE RELEVANCE OF SELF-CONTROL TO ACADEMIC SUCCESS

In the renowned ''Stanford marshmallow experiment,'' researchers found that four-year-olds who were most successful at delaying gratification when tempted with marshmallows or toys fared better in terms of social competence, academic success, and personal efficacy not only in their teenage years (Mischel, Shoda, & Rodriguez, 1989) but also into their adult years (Casey et al., 2011). In a typical scenario, a four- or five-year-old child would be offered one marshmallow. The child would then be told that if he (or she) could wait until the researcher returned a number of minutes later without eating the marshmallow, he would earn the right to have two marshmallows instead of just the one.

In multiple trials, the researchers tried many strategies to either enhance or hinder the children (Mischel et al., 1989). The children who were able to wait the longest without temptations or assistance were found to be more capable of handling social interactions, frustrations, and temptations as teenagers, according to parental ratings. In addition, they were more able as adults to express ideas, concentrate, plan ahead, and manage stress. Finally, those who had waited the longest as small children also achieved higher SAT scores as they prepared for college.

WHAT YOU CAN DO

- Teach students the strategies for maintaining worthwhile goals: a student might post a picture of himself or herself and the goal (together), do daily affirmations ("I can see it and feel it right now"), and track his or her goal progress in small increments.

- Teach students how to resist temptation. For example, show kids a real food treat (for example, a sweet). Then show kids a picture of the same treat. Ask them to close their eyes and see the real treat as a picture—and it will lose its appeal. Willpower is teachable!

- To reduce off-track behavior, give students "if-then"–type rules. Come up with two or three repeating scenarios in which your student gets frustrated. Create a rule for each one using a template along these lines: "When I see X happen, I'll always do Y." For example, let's say you have an important project to finish. When a friend says to you, "Hey, do you want to go to a movie?" do you have an immediate, rehearsed answer? If you do not have one, you may feel trapped and go do something that you actually would rather not do. Another example is, "Whenever I get a text message, then I will redirect my

energy to—and stay focused on—my task and bigger goal.''
Subjects struggled more with a less defined goal (''I won't
get distracted'') and stayed on track more when they had an
''if-then'' plan (Gawrilow, Gollwitzer, & Oettingen, 2011).

IMPROVING PROCESSING SKILLS

The word ''processing'' refers to the act of working with, modifying, or altering
something. When we say students are processing, we mean that they are doing
mental work. But processing is not an innate skill; it must be taught. Processing can
be done on a micro or macro level. At the micro level, small, tiny information ''bits''
are being altered by the students' brains. With auditory processing, students have
to learn how to distinguish between words like ''watch'' and ''wasp'' or ''boys''
and ''buoys,'' or they'll struggle with the essential building blocks of reading—the
phonemes. To help kids who struggle with auditory processing, consider using
a research-based auditory processing program, such as Fast ForWord, which has
extensive brain research behind it (Temple et al., 2003; Thibodeau, Friel-Patti, &
Britt, 2001). This program starts with brief and simple sounds in a video game
format. It uses extensive trial and error listening games requiring increasingly
complex and faster sounds to retrain the brain. But remember, kids will still
need to clearly buy into the program, setting compelling, self-directed goals for
maximum progress. When our brain gets invested in the learning, we work hard at
it with error correction, and we can make remarkable progress.

Five-Step Model for Teaching a Processing Skill

1 Model it by showing your students *how to do it.*

2 Debrief and *explain how* you just did it.

3 *Post the process that* you just modeled.

4 Give your students *a new problem* with guided practice.

5 Give students *independent practice* to solidify the process.

At the macro level, processing involves modifying or transforming symbols (words, numbers, logos, pictures, experiences, and so on) from one form into another. When a student summarizes a story, it is being processed. Processing also means dealing with a family argument, deciding what to do for the weekend, or building a fence. Writing down what you experienced is a processing skill. So is summarizing, and so is solving a problem. Many teachers notice when kids struggle with (or lack) these skills, but not enough teachers explicitly model and teach strong processing skills. Here are suggestions pertaining to several content areas:

WHAT YOU CAN DO

- Teach processing for every single content area. First, begin by introducing a relevant problem and get students to buy into the urgency of that problem. Next, use this simple five-step model: (1) model processing by showing students *how to do it*; (2) debrief and *explain how* you just did it; (3) *post the process* that you just modeled and explained; (4) give students a *new and similar problem* to solve with guided practice, providing additional error correction as needed; and finally, (5) give students *independent practice* to internalize the process. This will help kids learn how to think. Once they learn a new model, then let them practice it for a few weeks until they do it automatically.

- Many teach processing skills as a way to teach the writing process. For example, use these steps: (1) brainstorming, (2) prewriting, (3) completing the first draft, (4) sharing, (5) editing and rewriting, (6) proofreading, (7) completing the final draft, and (8) publishing. Reinforce these steps until students have them memorized. Flesh out each one of these, and then have students both write about the model, what they have learned, and when they would use it and teach their classroom peers.

- Teach processing steps for problems solving. To help students learn the model, give student pairs or teams the ten steps that follow *out of order*. Allow students six minutes to work with others to put the steps in the correct order. Once they do that, allow them another six minutes to give you an example of a problem they just solved using the model. Here are the ten steps, in order:

1. Have a positive attitude.
2. Identify the problem.
3. State the goal (reward).
4. Identify resources.
5. Review boundaries and limitations.
6. Identify potential paths.
7. Predict the risks.
8. Choose a strategy.
9. Implement and adapt the strategy.
10. Celebrate success.

- In math, teach the generic processing skills that are required to solve problems with the use of a problem-solving template. Create competition by breaking students into small teams. Each team uses a different problem-solving strategy, and also gets to pick a backup strategy. For a basic secondary-level math problem, here are some choices from which the team can pick before seeing the problem: (1) draw a diagram; (2) solve a simpler but similar problem, then guess; (3) work a problem backward first; (4) use a formula you already know; (5) use logical reasoning; (6) find a pattern; (7) make a table; (8) make a graph; or (9) start with a guess, then check work. All the student teams get nine minutes. Once the students finish their work, students from each team share their thinking with the class. Then let students develop their own "toolbox" of best strategies for solving math problems.

Processing skills, all of which are teachable, make up a broad category of thinking skills. When your kids don't know how to do something, they should break it down, write it out, and practice it over time. One-shot practice is not a skill builder, nor is simply giving information to your students. Use the five-step model shown earlier, and be sure to post the entire model for future reference. Continue to use this model over time. Less effective teachers teach a skill until kids get it right. Highly effective teachers work with kids until they can't get it wrong.

ATTENTION AND FOCUS

The brain will not change in response to direct instruction without the student's attention. As educators, we all know that when kids pay attention, cognitive activity usually goes up (Sarter, Gehring, & Kozak, 2006). Yet not all attention is the same, and the differences are critical. There are two primary types of attention; one is reactive and hardwired, and the other is reflective, learned, and earned.

Two Types of Attention

Hardwired and Reflexive	Reflective, Learned, and Earned
The student's brain automatically orients to danger, novelty, affiliation, contrast, movement, and risk-reward situations. *The capacity for sustaining this type of attention is naturally within all of us.*	This complex skill set requires the student to (1) disengage from the prior object of interest, (2) engage and focus on the new one, (3) suppress outside stimuli, and (4) stay engaged. *This type of attention takes practice!*

The first type of attention is the ''orient and focus'' that is hardwired. Instead of saying to students, ''Pay attention!'' what you really want to say is, ''Suppress interesting things!'' Why? Students already *do* pay attention. We're all designed by nature to orient and pay attention to moving objects, contrast, novelty, peers, or rapid environmental changes. Kids already notice another kid walking by or a peer making a gross sound. What you were hoping for was focus and suppression of outside distractions. As just alluded to, you'd make more sense if you said, ''Stop paying attention to biologically important but highly distracting things!''

The two types of attention remind us that there's only one you'll need to develop in your students. You want an academic focus, and for kids to remain ''locked in'' on the content every time. But that's a *learned* skill set. It takes ''practiced'' skills to suppress potentially distracting stimuli and continually orient to and focus on the content of the task. It takes musicians, writers, chess players, readers, and artists months or more commonly years to do that well. Telling kids to ''pay attention'' doesn't give them years of mental training. So what can be done in a classroom? First, stop expecting kids to pay extended, focused attention. They don't owe you anything. There are two solution types. The first is a work-around, which is a temporary solution. Examples of short-term solutions for attention building follow.

WHAT YOU CAN DO

- To boost attention, use prediction more thoughtfully and more often. Your students can a make prediction about something related to your content (the process, outcomes, circumstances, and so on). Then get them invested in their prediction by making the prediction public ("Raise your hand if you believe that such and such will turn out to be true"). Say, "Those who think such and such, please stand on the far side of the classroom. Those who think such and such stand over here." Next, increase the stakes of the prediction ("Those who predict correctly will get one free homework pass this month"). Then, find out who was right. Prediction forces the brain to care about the outcome because we get invested in being right.

- Use the "chunk and pause" technique. Every few minutes, give students a thirty- to ninety-second break so they can stand up, which will give them time to mentally process the content. Standing increases blood flow and may temporarily reduce postural stress. Then, reorient the students to the task.

- Prime the learning with small hints, appetizers, and teasers days or minutes ahead of time to create a pre-attentional bias toward the content.

- Develop an extra "hook" that fosters attentional vigilance (this strategy may appeal to learners' sense of risk, their preference for novelty, or their appreciation for friendships). "This next activity got the last teacher in a bit of trouble. But I think I have the kinks worked out. Let's see if we can pull it off.''

- Add a strong goal acquisition component to the activity (that is, make the goal worth achieving, such as via competition), and keep students invested in the target goal with public feedback, such as score-keeping.

- Do a fast physical activity (like Simon Says, with a student leading the class) first to activate executive function areas. The brain's internal focus-inducing chemical norepinephrine and working memory ally, dopamine, will both strengthen students' focus.

- Try "what's different?" activities. (These use two different pictures, both almost identical; the task is to find the differences.) Let kids create these with graphics programs and test each other in class. Begin with pictures that may have high teen interest, such as images of crowds of teens, and then move to pictures related to content.

You can build long-term attentional skills in many ways. High-interest reading material not only will engage kids but also will almost compel them to pay attention. ''Fast writes'' (save the editing for later) are a tool for developing focus.

Any of the following will strengthen long-term attentional skills: playing a musical instrument, creating artwork or designs, playing a sport and being coached, taking drama classes, or participating in dance training. These activities help students learn to orient their focus, pay attention, and suppress unwanted or irrelevant stimuli.

WORKING MEMORY

You may have kids who can't seem to follow directions or hold numbers in their head, or they may forget what they're reading as fast as they read it. These are common symptoms of a poor working memory. Research shows us that the strength of working memory is a predictor of student performance in attentional tasks (Fukuda & Vogel, 2009) and reasoning and problem solving (Barrouillet & Lecas, 1999). Working memory also can be used to predict performance in mathematics (De Smedt et al., 2009). In fact, a strong working memory is a greater predictor of academic success at age five than IQ (Alloway & Alloway, 2010).

What Is in Our Working Memory?

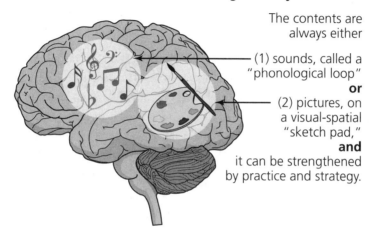

The contents are always either

(1) sounds, called a "phonological loop"
or
(2) pictures, on a visual-spatial "sketch pad,"
and
it can be strengthened by practice and strategy.

The great news is that working memory is teachable. Typical IQ tests are a combination of thinking, knowledge, and memory tasks. A key subskill being tested is working memory. In one recent study, working memory was strengthened over a period of nineteen days. This skill building actually boosted fluid IQ. In fact, the more hours of training students received, the greater the IQ effects (Jaeggi, Buschkuehl, Jonides, & Shah, 2011). This study provides further evidence that kids are not stuck with the intelligence they have. When you boost working memory, there is a wide range of other cognitive benefits. There are, however, some teachers who are stuck in their thinking. The idea is to be intentional about helping students build capacity.

WHAT YOU CAN DO

- Play games requiring learners to recall physical actions. For example, instead of using Simon Says as an energizer, you can use it as a working memory builder. "Simon says only follow the most recent command. Simon says stand up, *and* Simon says put your hands on your head." Then change it up a bit: "Simon says follow the first command and ignore the second. Simon says clap twice, and Simon says point to the exit sign." This way students have to ignore the current request and use an earlier one.

- Try the "file folder activity," which builds both working memory and listening skills. In this activity, students take turns saying words that come from the same "folder." For example, if the folder is countries, you can only say the names of countries and no other words. Students can start this activity with one partner (or in a team). In a pair, the person who goes first says a word from the folder, such as "Canada." The other partner repeats the word "Canada" and adds a new word from the same folder, such as "France." The first partner repeats, "Canada, France," and now adds a third country, like "Vietnam." This process goes on until someone is unable to add another country or cannot retrieve the previous ones. Teachers can use this game for five minutes a day in any content area as a pretest for prior knowledge or as a review. As students get better at the game, they can play in circles of five to eight students.

- Try "number add-ons," an exercise students can do as a whole class or in teams. In a process similar to that of the file folder game, a student calls out a number, and then the next student repeats that number and throws in an additional number. The student on his or her right does the same, repeating all numbers previously introduced. The first student might say "five," the second student "five, two," the third student "five, two, seven," and so on. Over time, you can modify this exercise by including larger numbers, adding processing to the numbers, or even stopping after a certain goal is reached.

- Switch working memory skill building from numbers to language arts or science. Put students in small groups (of four to five students each) and ask the first student to start with a "review sentence" pertaining to the current unit. The sentence has to be seven words or fewer. The second student repeats that sentence and adds a new sentence, and so on. Challenge students to see how far they can go. This activity builds attentional skills, working memory, and listening skills.

The right (and only) way to use working memory skill-building activities is to start small and build. Get buy-in at the beginning; keep the activity moving quickly, expanding it in small increments. Vary the types of tasks so that kids stay interested. Practice on existing classroom content in your current unit for ten minutes a day, three to five days a week, for eight to twelve weeks to see gains. These are not "filler" or "sponge" activities. You don't have time for that. Use this same protocol for all the skill-building activities in this chapter.

SEQUENCING SKILL BUILDERS

Sequencing involves multiple cognitive processes to put content in the correct order. To do laundry, one must fold clothes after they come out of the dryer and wash the clothes before drying them. These steps sound obvious, but they are only obvious once you've done the task. To sequence a task, you'll need background knowledge, the ability to prioritize, prediction skills, and speed of processing. Many students know what to do—they just don't know in which order to do it. As a result, they often end up struggling and often fail to complete tasks. You may have noticed in your own work how you constantly juggle tasks, which you mentally label as "urgent," "important," "delegate," or "save for later." If there are any gaps in your own cognitive processing, deadlines go unmet and someone ends up disappointed. In school, teachers often say something like "She's got her act together" when a student can prioritize and sequence tasks correctly.

WHAT YOU CAN DO

- Give students the opportunity to build things (models, paper projects, or project displays). Have them talk through what they're doing to help them learn how to sequence a task.

- Give kids directions for tasks only about 50 percent of the time or less. Every other time, list the five steps to a task up front, but put them in the incorrect order. Each student then works with a partner to get the right order.

- Encourage students to get involved in the arts. Most arts opportunities require attention, processing, and sequencing. For example, playing a song requires every note to be played in the correct order.

- Stop giving kids the task of writing a paragraph or short story (at least stop doing it 50 percent of the time). Instead, give students seven to eight sentences *out of order*. They work with a partner to figure out how to make a story out of it.

- Sequencing skills, like the other big five executive function skills, are teachable. Students need your guidance and plenty of experience and coaching. It also takes enough time for the brain to buy into the importance of sequencing, and to learn how to do it well. The sequencing activities just listed could become fun and challenging openers to the class.

RETURN TO GLORY

We began this chapter with the story of Marcus—a clear example of an individual with poor executive function. He acted a bit scattered at times, and had difficulty keeping on track and sustaining work on homework and projects. In short, his path wasn't working for him. In this case, a savvy teacher realized what was happening and sat down with Marcus to set up a plan. First, she told Marcus that brains can and do change. Brains are malleable and subject to life experiences. Change the experiences, and you change the brain. Marcus did not know that, and it got him motivated. Second, as part of their plan, Marcus took on special work for three days a week that focused on building executive function skills. Initially, these included study skills, organizational skills, and note-taking skills—all of which are critical "learn to learn" survival skills. We can see how Marcus was weak in the "big five" list items here:

1. **Self-control**: the capacity to restrain impulsivity

2. **Processing skills**: auditory, visual, and tactile

3. **Attentional skills**: the ability to engage, focus, and disengage as needed

4. **Memory capacity**: short-term and working memory

5. **Sequencing skills**: knowing the order of steps in a process

Finally, the more specific skills, such as mental computations, were built over a period of weeks and months, the most crucial of which had to do with improving working memory and attention. Marcus's teacher helped him develop these skills using the same strategies listed throughout this chapter. With your own students, start small with incremental increases in challenge levels and plenty of constructive feedback. Gradually add complexity and stay positive. The process required relentless focus on skill building. These skills can help any student become more competent, especially a student like Marcus. Within a few short weeks, Marcus could see and feel the difference. Although he's only considering going to college, at least he's thinking about it. There is no doubt, however, that he is going to graduate.

TO SUM UP

When students face the challenges described in this chapter, some educators dismiss them as being beyond help. That's a huge mistake. students' varying abilities, once believed to be inborn and immutable, have been shown to be shaped by both nature *and* nurture. Although there is a genetic basis for the abilities a student possesses, its influence is small compared to the influence of skill building. Remember, the heritability of any trait is unrelated to it's modifiability. Your students can change with your help. Daily experiences have the greatest influence on how the brain is built or neglected and how it functions throughout life. When you change the daily experiences, the brain will change. In substance, our cognition arises from countless interactions among a set of core mental processes. It's not unlike building with Legos. These complex cognitive structures are formed from simple pieces. Your daily work in skill building can allow you to see, hear, and feel the changes in your students—and you'll be able to see how changes in your students' mental habits can actually alter brain function.

When you help your students to think well, this fosters an impressive array of cognitive abilities they will have for a lifetime. Especially good news from all the research on brain changing and skill development is that one teacher can intervene positively and change a struggling student's life course. If you have made it this far in the book, you are probably excited about the possibilities. Maintain that excitement! Making changes in your teaching practice is hard work, but you can do it.

Model for your students what it looks like to take this path. Make changes in your teaching practice. If you don't try out new things, you rob your students of who they could be, and you rob yourself of who *you could be*. Focus on the what it will take to help your students succeed. Are you up for miracles? Your students are waiting for something miraculous!

Student Handout: Maximize Cognitive Capacity

- **Resist the temptation to procrastinate.** *Everyone is tempted to avoid schoolwork from time to time. You might be tempted to read only half of the assigned chapter or race through a set of math problems so you can go on Facebook. But this only makes it harder to keep going the next time. Instead, make a habit of working on assignments the day they are assigned—no matter what! After a while, the temptation to procrastinate will go away.*

- **Respect your "processing time."** *Processing time is how long it takes your brain to perform a cognitive task, like reading a passage, doing a math problem, or figuring out instructions on a worksheet. The more complicated the task, the longer the processing time. Break up assignments into bite-size pieces and give your brain enough time to process each piece, or step.*

- **Learn how to maintain attention and focus.** *A good way to learn how to maintain attention is, surprisingly, to give yourself scheduled breaks. Instead of sitting at a desk daydreaming and not making progress on your work, work intently for short periods, and then get up and walk around.*

- **Exercise the memory function of your brain.** *When a teacher asks you to memorize something—for example, a poem, math facts, or spelling words—make sure to do it and do it right! Using your memory is like a workout for your brain that you don't want to skip. Play memory games outside of school as well.*

- **Build cognitive sequencing skills.** *Almost every school assignment you receive will specify a proper sequence for completing it. When teachers tell you that you didn't follow directions, they often mean that you didn't do the steps in the correct order. Always study and commit to memory the instructions for performing an academic assignment.*

CHAPTER FIVE

FOSTER STUDENT EFFORT

Carson was a fifteen-year-old student who was struggling. Most teachers said motivation was his key issue. But lack of motivation is never a problem—it's a symptom. The question is, What is it a symptom of? In other words, What is the real problem? Teachers labeled Carson as another unmotivated teenager who needed to someday ''grow out of it.'' The consensus was simply to let him slide through school. They expected him to go through the motions and escape their class with a C or D grade. Unfortunately, this scenario occurs thousands of times each year—but it doesn't have to be this way, and at times something quite spectacular can happen instead. There are alternatives. This chapter will reveal one of the core attributes that you can foster: effort.

There's no shortage of theories about what makes students successful. Some parents and teachers believe that if students do their homework, they'll succeed. Others believe that the student's background is the greatest contributor to his or her success. We've all met those who believe gender, economic, or racial differences can have an impact on success. Some believe that birth order, the age of entering school, or the kind of school attended are the primary deciding factors. But those are unfounded beliefs. Of course, many will say that good, old-fashioned hard work is the primary factor in determining success.

All of us know that some kids may have hardships at home, a lower socioeconomic status, challenging emotional problems, and so on. Each of those is difficult in isolation, and some kids have many cards stacked against them. But remember, there are kids facing nearly impossible odds who succeed around the country because of just one teacher or counselor who refused to let them fail. When it comes to academic success, it is teachers who have a greater influence on how kids turn out than any other single variable, and their work contributes over 50 percent of how kids do academically (Hattie, 2010). You are vitally important to their success. We showed you that you can build cognitive capacity and improve attitude, and now we'll show how to foster effort.

THE BIG PICTURE OF SUCCESS

Teachers who foster effort (motivation, drive, and persistence) will develop students with a good chance at success. Effort is the sustained, raw energy over time that makes good things happen. Research supports task persistence as a huge factor in developing student success (Andersson & Bergman, 2011). In fact, the persistence and self-control to stick to a task matter twice as much as IQ (Duckworth & Seligman, 2005). Based on the research, there are some specific factors that teachers can influence that have a great impact on student effort.

We expect you to be familiar with some of the effort-building factors. For example, you may know that when you show more passion for learning, your students often want a piece of that passion and may try harder. Earlier, we introduced the potency of getting student buy-in before a task. Remember to use some of the specific buy-in strategies introduced in this book to hook students, and always build relevance. Make it "their idea" by providing some choice and control. Finally, stairstep the effort by starting with small, easy-to-manage "baby" steps. When they're ready for more, you'll know; they'll be hungry for it. Now, let's jump into some of the most researched factors that you should know about.

HIGH-RETURN EFFORT BUILDERS

Ongoing research has targeted the classroom factors that have the biggest impact in terms of boosting effort and student learning. Each item listed here is known as a "high-yield factor" because it provides a huge return on your effort in terms of student achievement (Hattie, 2010). The top seven factors in supporting student effort are presented here in no specific order:

- Ongoing formative assessment
- High engagement with reciprocal (peer) teaching

- Teacher-student and student-student relationships

- Teaching for mastery with clarity and challenge

- Comprehensive, targeted interventions

- Class climate and high expectations

- Continuous, informal feedback

We will expand further on these factors throughout this chapter so they become more actionable at school. Each of them will help you reach your students. As you read this chapter, make a mental note of which ones you consider to be areas of existing strength for you, and which ones are opportunities for you to sample and try new approaches. These factors are not grouped in any specific order, so treat them as equally important.

ONGOING FORMATIVE ASSESSMENT

Teachers who use formative assessments get more effort out of students. Such assessments tell the teacher exactly what needs to happen next for a given student to succeed. With that information, teachers can plan and quickly implement interventions to keep students excited about succeeding. When conducting a formative assessment, you are using the evidence of learning (or lack of it) to adjust instruction. A review of research (Black & Wiliam, 1998) concluded that regular use of classroom formative assessment has the potential to raise student achievement by a substantial level, from 0.4 to 0.7 standard deviations. You may know that a standard deviation is a statistical measure that tells you the "spread" of the data. The more spread out the data, the greater the standard deviation that each person might be from another. See the box that follows for details on effect sizes. In other longer-term (twelve months or more) implementation studies, researchers have found smaller effect sizes—typically around 0.30 (William, Lee, Harrison, & Black, 2004)—but even those are still noticeable effects. Hattie (2003, 2010) found formative assessment to be in the top three factors for enhancing student achievement. Formative assessment has been found to be effective across many variables (student ages, the duration used, and the frequency used), and even when used for special needs populations.

FORMATIVE ASSESSMENT FACTORS AND THEIR RELATED EFFECT SIZES

Effect Size is a standard measure of the *relative size of the gain (or loss)* of an intervention.

> 0.00 or less = Negative effects
> 0.00–0.20 = Negligible, unclear effects
> 0.20–0.40 = Small–moderate effects
> 0.40–0.60 = Very strong effects
> 0.60–2.00 = Extreme effects

This is just one way of understanding the value of educational/classroom factors. There are others.

Effect sizes below 0.40 are considered minimal.

- **Diagnosis feedback: 0.52**

- **Mastery learning (based on feedback): 0.50**

- **Remediation and feedback: 0.65**

- **Corrective feedback: 0.94**

- **Feedback and reinforcement of learning: 1.13**

Source: **Adapted from Hattie & Timperley, 2007.**

What exactly is formative assessment? It is the measuring of progress against a bar or standard in a continuous process. Progress could be measured by the use of quizzes, student-generated graphic organizers, project learning, checklists, or rubrics. The bottom line is that this process is designed to generate evidence as to where student learning is, and whether the learning is on or off track. When teachers actively seek real evidence of the effects of their work, they are left asking, ''Now what?'' This can generate new hypotheses about what is or is not working, in turn leading to the introduction and use of newly adjusted and more effective strategies. This is how the ideal education process should work: teach, assess, learn, adapt, and reassess. If you don't know *where students are today*, you're teaching in the dark. When *you're in the dark*, your students lose interest and effort drops.

WHAT YOU CAN DO

- Begin with a mind-set of asking, "Do I know where my students are every day, or at least every week?" You cannot expect a strong student effort when your own effort is directed elsewhere. Know where your students are, then make corrections.

- Establish a clear (very clear!) student starting benchmark at the beginning of a unit. This can be done by (1) asking students to write a paragraph or two about their current understanding of the material to be taught, (2) creating a checklist for students to find out what they know, or (3) administering a pretest.

- Have your students develop a rubric, with your input, that delineates the components of high-quality work. Your contribution to this process is important because they must start the year with not only their personal understanding of quality but also your own standards. Let them measure their work against the rubric often, and make course adjustments to get their work to match the standards.

- Use student-created quizzes, which are another solid version of formative assessment. Students work in small teams or with partners to generate questions pertaining to a body of content, as well as the answers. Their questions will have to fit preset criteria and be vetted either by you or by other students.

HIGH ENGAGEMENT WITH RECIPROCAL (PEER) TEACHING

The second of seven effort builders is engagement. Continuous classroom engagement consistently ranks high as a contributor to student achievement (Marks, 2000). Engagement comes in many forms: simple physical engagement (stretching), social engagement (through partner work or team projects), and engagement in thinking processes and questioning strategies, among others. Engagement does not have to be only in the form of high-level cognitive processing to be valuable: keeping learners in engaging, productive emotional states is critical to their having a positive school experience (Reyes, Brackett, Rivers, White, & Salovey, 2012).

In fact, engagement can instill in students feelings of anticipation, curiosity, and excitement. The more quality minutes per day of learning, the more productive class time is for students. One of the most persistent complaints from teens is that "school is boring." In contrast, the evidence is strong that ongoing classroom engagement avoids the boredom issue and fosters learning with robust contributions to achievement (Appleton, Christenson, & Furlong, 2008; Ladd & Ladd, 2009). Kids who are engaged simply put out more effort.

THE MORE YOU TELL THEM, THE LESS THEY TRULY LEARN

Engage more and talk less.

Reciprocal teaching can strengthen engagement and, ultimately, student achievement (Rosenshine & Meister, 1994). This instructional process builds capacity among students with a simple template: the teacher first gets student buy-in, and then introduces a new cognitive strategy, such as prediction. The teacher's modeling the concept is critical so that the students see how the activity should be done. Students will move from a passive role to an active role by having a chance to teach the newly learned content. In this process, the students take turns assuming the teacher role to share their understanding of the content with their peers through a dialogue. Students also check their own understanding by generating questions and summarizing. The effect size for reciprocal teaching is a huge 0.74, putting it in the top ten most effective teacher strategies, according to Hattie (2010). Engagement may be simple or complex; it can be fostered solo, in pairs, in teams, or with the whole class. It can be more physical, emotional, social, or cognitive. Engagement can happen when seated, when standing, with movement, or outside the classroom. In short, the possibilities and combinations are endless.

WHAT YOU CAN DO

- Start with something simple, such as a "follow the leader" activity. Students are in small groups (or teams), and they pick a leader. The leader takes a walk around the room, showing off a dance move, playing an imaginary sport, such as tennis, or running and maybe occasionally clapping or changing directions (moving safely and within reason). That leader's group or followers will mimic the same moves. Use music to strengthen the fun mood. This activity should take forty-five seconds. Then, ask students to return to their seat.

- Ask students to write about what they have learned. Start with brainstorming and word association to generate a list of key words. Then have them input that list into a graphic organizer, independently or in pairs. Use categories that will help students think about their topic in challenging ways. Once the graphic organizer is done, ask students to summarize what they have learned in two paragraphs. They can then trade papers with each other to begin the process of peer editing.

- To facilitate reciprocal teaching, pick a key skill you'd like to teach, such as how to summarize a page or chapter. First, model the process and list no more than five steps. Then, tell students to generate questions to ask about how specifically they would perform the task and the ideal specs of the final product. After clarification, let students try it out, each taking a turn acting as a mentor or tutor for a partner. Then debrief the learning with a student-generated rubric.

TEACHER-STUDENT AND STUDENT-STUDENT RELATIONSHIPS

The third of seven effort builders is relationships. Think back to your own experiences of school, and to all the teachers you had. When you liked a teacher, did you tend to work harder for him or her? The value of positive relationships with your students, although not universal, cannot be overstated. Research suggests that this variable consistently ranks over 0.60 in effect size, meaning it is significant and powerful. Hattie's research (2010) ranks it as a high-yield difference-maker with a considerable 0.72 effect size. Anything over 0.40 is considered moderate to substantial. Quality relationships with students can lower their stress and provide hope for them when it comes to their chances for success. Behavioral role models provide support for students when they are struggling. Further, students who like their teacher are simply more likely to work harder for him or her.

WHAT YOU CAN DO

- Learn something every day about your kids. Ask yourself, "What do I really know about this student?" Do you know anything about the student's family? Do you know how many siblings he or she has, or who lives with him or her? Do you know about the student's interests, hobbies, and passions? These might provide a source for making connections between the student's life and the content you are teaching.

- Make sure you know all students by name, and refer to them by name in class. Offer regular opportunities in class for students to "meet and greet others in class" as a fringe benefit of a learning activity. For example, they might interact with each other in this way as part of a team-building process or a "think-pair-share" activity. Check in with students daily via a class walkabout.

- Honor the uniqueness of and differences among students in your class, and help students do the same. Ask each student to write a one-page autobiography. Students are to write about three things that changed their lives the most (their parents' divorce, winning something, making a team or a friendship, and so on). When students share these autobiographies with the class, it has the potential to create respect and lead to bonding.

TEACHING FOR MASTERY WITH CLARITY AND CHALLENGE

The fourth of seven effort builders is teaching for mastery with clarity and challenge. Students generally love to learn at a greater level of quality, depth, and meaning (versus quick, shallow, for-the-test learning). Over eighty thousand secondary students were asked, "If you have been bored in class, why?" The top answer was that the material wasn't interesting (75 percent). But almost one-third of all high school students complained that the work wasn't challenging enough (Yazzie-Mintz, 2010).

They needed challenge! Without sufficient challenge, effort stops. You might say that when a teacher gets the students to learn the material, "That's just good teaching." But when it comes to mastery, there is no *just good enough*. The "win" comes from the process of developing mastery, not the destination. It's the "thrill of the chase" that makes complex, challenging learning worthwhile. The effect size of this factor is considerable, with 0.75 for teacher clarity and 0.58 for teaching students for mastery versus teaching them to acquire the basics only. This type of teaching requires a savvy, hands-on style and constantly giving students feedback.

BRAINS RARELY GET IT RIGHT THE VERY FIRST TIME EXPECT TO CORRECT & ACCURACY WILL CLIMB

Expect to correct.

Teaching for mastery is different from teaching simply to cover the content. Seeking mastery typically starts with setting very high, challenging goals—ones that the student will initially wonder if he or she is capable of reaching at all. The instructor who is teaching for mastery says, ''I don't just want them to get it right. I want to inspire them to become so proficient that they can't get it wrong. Only then will we move on.'' Savvy teachers teach the same thing multiple ways, using feedback, fresh strategies, and formative assessment to guide their error correction. They ensure kids have the skills to go to more complex, challenging levels, such as mastery. Ineffective teachers, by contrast, teach their content with little feedback from teacher to student or from student to teacher. They finish with little or no formative assessment.

WHAT YOU CAN DO

- Keep the learning targets visually displayed in the room, front and center. Tell students that they can achieve the posted learning goals, and that you'll be there to help them. Provide clarity and support!

- Never overfocus on any one strategy. Instead, use rotating strategies. You might include models, video, hands-on work, worked examples, peer tutoring, positive and extended questioning strategies, and reciprocal teaching.

- Combine graphics with verbal descriptions. If you don't have a needed graphic, search for an image on Google (respecting copyrights) or have students draw one. Continually connect and integrate abstract and concrete representations of concepts.

- At the beginning of each class, ask students to take a moment to write out and then turn in a quick graphic organizer depicting the previous day's learning. This allows you to provide clear feedback and demonstrates your high expectations—and it both leads to memory consolidation among students and promotes student engagement.

- On a daily basis, look for substantive errors (using formative assessment). One teacher I knew of asked his students to copy down each day's new lesson at the outset. They drew out a fresh graphic organizer using lines, arrows, and pictures to show the relationships within the content, properties of key elements or forces, and the core content.

- Interweave worked example solutions and problem-solving exercises. Help students build content explanations (who, what, how, why, when, where) by having them ask and answer deep questions. Teach students the power of compelling questions. In math, start the day with a review of the prior day's teaching in front of the class (stretch out the learning as much as possible), meaning you'll be using priming and reviews while doing error correction (giving feedback). To build a class climate of excellence, never let students go more than twenty-four hours with a wrong answer or misconception. When students work hard to get complex content learned, it's a learning "high."

COMPREHENSIVE, TARGETED INTERVENTIONS

We've all recognized the fallacy of the expression "One size fits all," particularly when it comes to teaching. Behind this understanding is the entire "differentiation" movement, which asks teachers to learn to tier instruction and curriculum up or down to meet the needs of all students. The data clearly show that targeted small group instruction has a huge positive effect on student achievement. The strong effect size ranges from 0.77 to 0.88 (Hattie, 2010), depending on which students are included in the study (regular education students, special education students, and other student groups). These, again, are strong, top ten effect sizes and are considered huge by any measure. Teachers should allot part of their time to focused interventions with students who need particular help.

The most common interventions are capacity builders. This category encompasses a large assortment of skills, including such typical areas of executive function as processing, self-control, sequencing, organizing, or working memory as well as content areas that may focus on catching up in such areas as vocabulary, math, and reading. If there's a gap identified by the teacher or appropriate assessments, the teacher can target, focus on, and succeed in filling that gap. The results of the intervention can be miraculous. In classrooms with high-performing teachers, the students who need an intervention are more likely to be identified, and the teachers are more likely to use the key interventions that students might need to succeed, as shown by testing. The positive effect of "microteaching" on a student's self-concept and expectations can be enormous.

WHAT YOU CAN DO

- Identify underperforming students and work with them in small groups of one to four on specific skills or attitude building. This can be done before class, during class if others are busy, and after class.

- Target fewer cognitive skills (these are addressed in Chapter Four), and teach them thoroughly. For example, working memory practice should go on for eight to twelve weeks to become solid.

- Use this intervention time to focus simultaneously on other, noncognitive skills. You can be building social skills in parallel with the cognitive ones.

CLASS CLIMATE AND HIGH EXPECTATIONS

Class climate is never an accident. It is built, for better or for worse, through a complex and often invisible array of brain-changing strategies. Daily comments, experiences, and activities slowly inch up or inch down students' perceptions of themselves, their goals, and their expectations. Occasionally a teacher will complain that a student "has an attitude" or seems "unmotivated" to learn. Typically, expert-level teachers create a climate in which students develop better attitudes. In short, instead of complaining about *what* kids don't have or don't do correctly, the high-performing teachers teach kids *how* to do the skills. How important is this difference? The effect size of students' having expectations for themselves is "off the charts" high at 1.44 (Hattie, 2010).

As teachers, we could say that students' expectations come more from the students than from teachers, but in truth, kids are not particularly sophisticated or purposeful in managing their own beliefs. Teachers have much more to do with student attitudes than they think. This is good news. You have considerable control when it comes to influencing students' predictions about their own path. Your class climate is a daily salad in which you have located the ingredients, prepped them, arranged them, and served them. In a positive climate of academic optimism, students believe they can achieve high standards. Kids need to feel challenged and enjoy the learning, because the emotional climate strongly correlates with the level of academic achievement (Reyes et al., 2012).

When a teacher thinks that a student is an "attention deficit/hyperactivity disorder kid" or a "troubled kid," it can work against both the teacher and the student. For example, when teachers are not labeling students, it ranks an impressive 0.61 in effect size contributing to student achievement (Hattie, 2010). Not labeling means expectations are high for every kid, not just the ones who show quick promise.

Extensive research into emotional climate suggests there is a positive-to-negative ratio for optimal learning success that helps each of us perform our best in learning (Fredrickson & Losada, 2005). When it comes to class climate, most teachers don't track the ratio of positive to negative interactions, such as affirmations versus reprimands. Maybe they should. Too many positives may lead to kids' getting spoiled. Too many negatives may contribute to resistance and a foul mood in regard to learning. Use the 3:1 ratio of positives to negatives. The hope-building climate fostered by such a ratio is powerful in generating greater student achievement (Rand, 2009; Zimmerman, 1992).

When determining a student's level of motivation, we are also holding up a mirror to the ways we have touched or not touched his or her life. The student's motivation and expectations are in large part a reflection of the teacher's efforts. For example, although there are countless ways teachers could answer students' questions, those who create a positive climate find ways to affirm curious students and challenge them to reach higher. The combination of all of these microeffects creates either a neutral, negative, or positive class climate in which students will either behave in motivated ways or become increasingly uninterested. Yes, you do make a difference—a big one! When effort is up, when emotions are positive, you have a classroom environment in which effort is contagious. Here's how you can get more effort in your classroom climate.

WHAT YOU CAN DO

- Although you may not track the exact ratio of positive to negative interactions, remember that if you had to discipline a student on a given day, engage in three positive interactions with that student before he or she goes home. Research shows that initiating or participating in three positive interactions for each reprimand works best.

- Do not ask students to put down "doing their personal best" as a goal. That's usually too low. Set high course goals and help students get to them. Students can set "microgoals" within the bigger goals.

- Lower the risk so that students feel safer in putting out the effort to respond. When students contribute, instead of responding with a "Hmm, okay . . .," post up and use these rules: "Everyone participates at least once a day, every day, in class. This means you'll get thanked by me for every response and (1) volunteer a question or comment, (2) respond when called on, or (3) write out a written content question and give it to me as a "door pass" before you go.

- To boost classroom engagement and to get higher effort, use the "two rounds" for questions. In Round 1 (reactive), questions are quick surveys to find out what students think a correct first response might be. In Round 1, everyone raises their hand and jumps in. In Round 2, students get up to one minute to answer the same question, but this time, it's on a deeper collaborative level. They can talk with a neighbor and reflect on their answers. Both of the two types of answers will get more effort. Why? In the first round, every student is thanked, right or wrong. Here's how Round 1 works:

    If you call on a student in class and he or she gives you an answer to your question, thank the student for his or her effort and participation—whether or not the student got the answer right. Do not tell the student whether he or she got it right or wrong. If you want more effort from kids, start giving positive feedback every single time they take a risk. Use the following types of responses to Round 1 student guesses: "Thank you." "Love the effort" or "Good enthusiasm, who else?" "Thanks for contributing" or "Thanks; let's check in with a few others." You'll notice that every single one of these responses focuses on the *effort*, not on the substance. In Round 1, never, ever say "good" or "fantastic" unless you specifically qualify the word with a mention of effort (for example, "Good effort—thanks!"). Otherwise, you'll confuse your students ("Hmm . . . did the teacher's 'Good!' refer to the answer I gave, or my effort?"). Students may give inappropriate answers on purpose, just to see if you'll get discombobulated. The better you maintain your "cool," the less students will try to get you off balance. Round 1 is all about appreciating the effort and risk. From that perspective, every student contribution (within ethical and tasteful boundaries) is acceptable as an effort. When you reinforce effort, you get more of it.

This strategy does three things: (1) it will get kids to feel "safe" about contributing to your class and lead them to become more confident; (2) it will get far more hands to go up; and (3) it gives you feedback on what a large number of kids know because you ask five, ten, or twenty kids each time.

How else can you get students to respond to you in Round 1? If the student is NOT READY and you call on him or her, the student can say: "I'd like a time lifeline" (giving the student up to a minute before having to respond) or "I'd like to consult a neighbor." In this case, you'll check back with the student in a moment. If the student has NO CLUE, he or she can say, "I don't know, but I'd like to know." In that case you call on the next student.

- Tell students that something may be challenging, but they will have your support as they learn it and master it.

- Use music and positive energizers with more movement and celebrations to keep the physical and mental energy high as you show a real passion for teaching.

CONTINUOUS, INFORMAL FEEDBACK

Feedback is one of the single most powerful factors ever discovered to influence student effort and achievement. The average effect size is an enormous 0.79 (Hattie, 2010). To place this score into perspective, feedback is a top ten factor in nearly every meta-study done on student achievement (Hattie & Timperley, 2007). Studies showing that feedback is less effective are typically ones in which the primary feedback is in the form of praise, reward, or punishment. In contrast, feedback studies showing the greatest effect sizes used feedback in its ideal form: students received specific, factual feedback about their work on the task at hand, and it was instructive enough to help them do that work more effectively.

We define the term *student feedback* as information provided by any agent, be it a teacher, student, event, process, book, outsider, and so on, as a consequence of performance as measured against a standard. If the feedback is received by the teacher from the student, it is still information that the teacher receives about how the student or the teacher is doing measured against their goals. Whereas 70 percent of teachers insist that they provide plenty of feedback to students, only 45 percent of students agree with this assertion (Carless, 2006). Many administrators and teachers often use testing to judge *whether or not* change has occurred. What students need is actionable feedback. If quality feedback were given, it would clearly signal *how* to alter or strengthen the learning so that they could do something differently the next time.

Students are brought through a system in which the most used markers of progress, federal and state tests, are never used in instructive ways with actionable debriefing. The costs of the mandated right-wrong accountability tests are significant, and unfortunately the feedback that students should get is typically nonexistent (Shepard et al., 1996). Although this issue may be out of a teacher's hands, the feedback that students get in the classroom can be improved significantly. To maximize the value of the feedback you provide, keep it nonpersonal. Avoid such phrases as "You didn't try hard." Instead, say, "Here's what to look for and complete differently next time." Then ensure that students have bought into the task they're doing—feedback should address the gap between the work at hand and students' goals. "The reason your equation didn't work out is this: remember to put the XY on the right side of the equation because it eliminates the uncertainty of the Z value" is an example of quality feedback.

School (and later on, jobs) require extraordinary amounts of detail, and there are high stakes in regard to getting answers correct. But humans over the last two thousand years could live just fine making reasonably good guesses. The human brain is best designed to get the gist of things, not fine detail. There's no evidence that the brain is inherently good at learning the extraordinary details of content that might be found in a typical school setting, much of which may seem irrelevant to survival. This shift, from being academically "close" to getting endless arrays of academic detail correct, is one that strong teachers can orchestrate. To get from a "rough draft" version of learning in our brain to an accurate understanding, it typically takes considerable feedback. There's a reason this factor is rated so highly; without receiving feedback, we're only guessers. We know that all kids learn from both positive and negative performance feedback. We also know that feedback is a core foundational piece of a successful learning scaffold. And we know that feedback has no effect in a vacuum—it must be given in the context of support in the classroom and goal-directed learning.

Certain types of feedback are better than others. Feedback is the most powerful when it is generated by students and given to the teacher. When teachers gain feedback from students telling them precisely where students are, what they know and don't know, as well as the source of student errors, only then can teachers adapt and alter their teaching to better facilitate student learning. Without continuous feedback, teachers might as well be teaching with a bag over their head. They simply cannot make wise decisions quickly enough to meet the students' needs.

WHAT YOU CAN DO

- Use quizzing to promote learning. Quizzes, generated either by you or by your students, are a helpful means of giving and getting feedback.

- Give immediate, uncomplicated cues or reinforcement to learners. These can be in the form of video, pictures, sounds, or text—or even computer-assisted instructional feedback.

- Use variety. Regardless of the type of feedback, students may become desensitized to it and it may lose value. Rotate your feedback so that you use different types on different days.

- Feedback can be anything that helps fill the "gap" between where a student is now and where the goal is. Therefore, feedback may be about effort ("I appreciate your good, sustained effort"); about strategy ("That quick change you made worked out well, didn't it?"); or about attitude ("You seemed really excited about trying this out").

- The strongest feedback relates progress or the lack of it directly to the mutually agreed-on goal ("Right now you're 80 percent finished. How are you going to get the rest done on time?"). The student has to both receive the feedback and act on it ("Are you on the right path, or do you need to change anything?"), and you may need to add some additional motivation, framing, or cognitive perspective to increase receptivity to midcourse corrections. In short, feedback must be received within the context of a positive relationship, and it must be given with knowledge of the student, the context, the goals, and the content.

- Make the feedback accurate, not vague. One researcher found that most of the feedback that students got was vague, incorrect, and from other unsure students (Nuthall, 2005). This means you should ensure (using checklists, coaching, rubrics, or computer assistance) that kids get accurate feedback. When you use peers as a source of feedback you should build the structure for feedback, set up a positive classroom frame, and delineate the quantity of feedback as well as the attitude to be used with the activity so that peers know exactly how to give feedback.

THE REST OF THE STORY

Carson, the adolescent male introduced at this chapter's outset, was struggling in school. He just didn't feel like trying much at all. But things turned around. How? A savvy teacher saw his lethargy and lack of motivation as symptoms, not the problem. The teacher who succeeded with Carson was simply unwilling to "kick the can down the road" and hope that someday Carson would "grow out of it." What did the teacher actually do?

The first thing the teacher did was establish and strengthen a relationship with Carson. The teacher posed questions over time to Carson, such as "What do you care about? Who is in your family? What events have happened recently in your life that matter to you?" The first thing that emerged in the time Carson and the teacher spent building a relationship was a surprise. The teacher found out that Carson's dad was killed in the Middle East conflict. Such losses are difficult for any family member, but adolescent males are particularly affected. Carson really needed a trusting, caring adult to connect with him, not just dismiss him as a "lost teenager."

Next, the teacher began to use some of the effort-building factors mentioned in this chapter. All work was highly engaging and personal and included feedback. Carson was offered time to practice skill building because his working memory was weak, and so were his attentional skills. Once his skills began to grow, his attitude started to shift. He could tell a teacher cared, he was seeing results, and he began to think about the possibilities in his future. Motivation picked up. There was no one "magic bullet" that the other teachers had been hoping for. The process was slow and steady, with no giving up, yet something quite spectacular began to happen. Build the relationship, build skills, allow hope to flourish, and build the growth mind-set to foster big thinking. This formula does not apply to all kids, but it worked well for Carson.

TO SUM UP

This chapter showed that student effort is not fixed; you can influence it. We are led to see that there are no stuck students. There are only teachers who are stuck and give up on kids. Are you now psyched up, or are you "sitting on the fence" about whether student effort is genetically based or influenced by teaching? If you're on the fence, what do you need to get down from it and pick the side called, "This is doable; I can now build effort"? We have now explored how to build attitude, capacity, and effort. In upcoming chapters, we'll introduce you to how to reach exceptional students; how to get strategic about goal setting; as well as how to strengthen body, mind, and soul.

Remember, most kids are only in school for just a few reasons: mainly, because it's the law and their friends are there. But they are not stuck where they are. Their success is dependent on the commitment of their teachers and the powerful, sustained interventions used. Each day, our brains adapt to our experiences. There's a chicken-and-egg effect happening. We change our brains, and our changed brains change us. This means that if you think of your students as simply needing a nudge to take the first step in the right direction, you can get pretty far. That immediate success step then changes students' perceptions about their future. Maybe they feel a bit more hopeful, so they try harder. The cycle of success has now begun: get a little success, then reinforce it, debrief it, and go for another success. Does this mean that every single student is reachable? We don't know. But we do know that we can reach many, many more.

Student Handout: Maximize Effort

- **Become an engaged learner**. *If you sit in the classroom passively waiting for the teacher to fill your head with knowledge, you will only get more and more bored. Be proactive. Force yourself to raise your hand. Force yourself to ask questions and take notes even when you aren't directed to do so. Think about what you are learning and try to make connections to other subjects and areas of your life. You will be surprised at how small efforts like this will change your experience at school.*

- **Be a teacher as well as a student**. *When you know something, share it! Explaining complicated tasks to others helps you to learn the task you are explaining even better. Teaching a subject or concept allows you to take your understanding to a whole new level.*

- **Build relationships with teachers and other students**. *Get to know your teachers and fellow students. Don't be an island unto yourself! When you feel connected to others, you can't help but put forward the extra effort. Strong relationships can foster a positive learning community in your classroom.*

- **Don't be satisfied with just understanding a subject—master it**. *Many students stop working when they reach the minimum understanding of a subject. They tell themselves that's all they have to do. But if you push yourself to understand everything you can about a subject, recognizing connections to other subjects and going beyond the textbook, you'll be surprised at how easy it is to get high grades and have fun at the same time.*

- **Be the solution in a chaotic classroom, not part of the problem**. *We all know that it's easy to laugh when the class clown acts up. And laughing once in a while is no crime. Recognize, however, that even if you are not causing disruptions, you have a choice about how you will respond. Your response can make the difference between a classroom environment that supports learning and one in which very little learning can occur.*

CHAPTER SIX

EMPOWER EXCEPTIONAL LEARNERS

Jason was a good kid. It's just that everything he touched turned to trouble. His homework was rarely turned in. If it was submitted, it was rarely on time. He often offended others, even though he had a ''good heart.'' He put in the effort, but things took interminably long. The teachers kept telling him about all of his ''potential'' (''Don't we all have potential?''). Jason was an exceptional learner, defined as ''not mainstream.'' And unless you can recognize learners like Jason quickly and adapt just as rapidly, they are likely to continue to struggle. Jason had a teacher just like you. His teacher had to figure out the ''puzzle'' of what was going on and come up with a solution to it.

You may have students like Jason, and it's easy to get frustrated with them. Just for a moment, however, think of exceptional, misbehaving, or underperforming students as mysteries to solve rather than problems. When dealing with such learners, highly effective teachers show willingness to look for clues beneath the surface. This chapter will help you begin your own search for clues. If we want ALL kids to graduate, and if we want to build capacity in ALL students, we'll want to consider the exceptional ones.

Exceptional learners are often known as the outliers. These might be kids from poverty, kids with special needs, kids who underperform, and kids who are labeled as ''gifted,'' among others. Naturally, you could have students with any combination of qualities *from within* those groups of outliers, too. First, we'll answer a critical question: What proportion of students are exceptional? The natural follow-up questions are, What do we know about those kids? How can we serve them better? and certainly, What can we learn about working with these learners that will shift their success rate upward dramatically? We'll address each of those questions in this chapter, and we will share some powerful, research-based strategies for supporting their long-range goals in Chapter Eight. The two types of exceptional students we'll be exploring are

- Academically gifted students (learners showing high ability or high IQ, which includes kids with disabilities or from poverty)

- Academically challenged students (including students with behavior issues, students with special needs, and students from poverty)

Here are some signs that you may be teaching an exceptional learner:

- **Head movement**. Notice extra head turning, which could be a sign of auditory processing deficits. The student may be trying to pick up auditory cues from others.

- **Impulsivity**. Exceptional learners may blurt out words or phrases, raise their hand before they have the answer, jump to conclusions, and seem jumpy. These behaviors could indicate attention deficits or symptoms of a stress disorder, occurring in well over 25 percent of kids (Evans & Kim, 2012; Kilpatrick & Saunders, 1997).

- **Forgetfulness**. Notice the student's inability to ''hold'' things in his or her head. When reading, the student might forget the first half of the sentence before he or she has finished the rest. In math, having the student keep one number in his or her head is fine—but ask the student to add, subtract, multiply, and so on, and the numbers may seem to ''fall out'' of his or her head (possibly indicating working memory issues).

- **Boredom**. Students who are playing; acting out; talking to others; or doing off-task, nonacademic work at their desk during class time may be gifted learners who are finding the pace of the learning, the topic, or the level of difficulty to be remarkably unsuited to their brain, or they may be struggling students who can't keep up and are frustrated.

The truth this, these factors are present every day in most classes for some students. But they don't have to be. When you give students the help they need, it changes their academic life. Exceptional learners could have an amazing, enriching day, every day—and this chapter will begin to show how you could help bring about this outcome.

WHO ARE TODAY'S "TYPICAL" STUDENTS?

In most schools, kids might attend regular education, gifted education, or special education classes. In some cases, they are placed in an inclusive class that combines the students. In reality, how different from each other are these students? We see that teachers are constantly asked to use "differentiation" strategies in class. But who is a typical student and who is exceptional? Neuroscientists at UCLA have been collecting brain data from around the world to find out what is "typical." To go about this research, they prescreened every possible research subject through (1) a detailed telephone interview, (2) in-person personal history gathering, and (3) a physical examination. Their goal was to exclude from the study any participants who were not likely to have a healthy, "typical" brain—such as those with a history of head trauma, high blood pressure, violence, long-term medication use, or drug abuse. They scanned thousands of healthy, "normal" human brains across the human age span using structural and functional brain imaging data. Because the scientists had an existing database of over thirty thousand scans, they had used it to determine how much the new subjects varied from those having the "typical" human brain scan.

In seeking to discover what the "typical" or "normal" brain looked like, here's what they found: the so-called typical, healthy brain is the exception (Mazziotta et al., 2009). The "take-home" message from this study is that differences (the exceptions) are the norm! By the way, the science is solid on this: this study was published in a prestigious, peer-reviewed scientific journal by pioneers in the brain-imaging field, John Mazziotta and Arthur Toga. Between the two of them, they have authored over six hundred journal articles. The myth of the typical brain means that the whole triangle model of who is "typical" (we used to think that was the majority) and who is not (we used to think the number was about 10 percent) can be turned upside down. In short, the majority of kids would not pass as having a healthy brain; and we might want to rethink our notion of a "healthy person," given that only 11 percent qualified for that designation in this study.

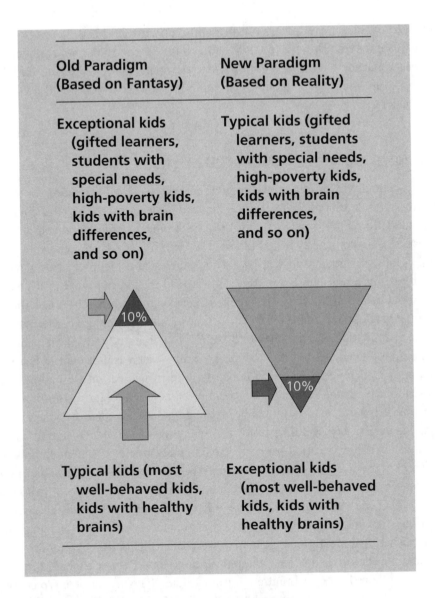

Old Paradigm (Based on Fantasy)	New Paradigm (Based on Reality)
Exceptional kids (gifted learners, students with special needs, high-poverty kids, kids with brain differences, and so on)	Typical kids (gifted learners, students with special needs, high-poverty kids, kids with brain differences, and so on)
Typical kids (most well-behaved kids, kids with healthy brains)	Exceptional kids (most well-behaved kids, kids with healthy brains)

WHAT MAKES LEARNERS EXCEPTIONAL?

What makes us who we are is a combination of genes and environment. Genes are not our destiny. Yes, they can code for eye, hair, and skin color; a narrow selection of diseases; and a few other qualities—but genes are only part of the equation. Our genes are also extracting information from the environment, and they respond to events outside the body. The ''nature-nurture'' debate is outdated because both genes and environment interact with each other.

Humans share over 99 percent of the same genes. Yet within any two humans (think of your students), certain of these identical genes may be "expressed" in one and not expressed in another. The expression or suppression of a gene's capacity may make the difference for parents between having a child with healthy muscle development and having a child with muscular dystrophy. The factors that influence gene expression include social conditions, exercise, new learning, stress, and variations in physical and social environments. In short, there's no limit to the capacity for variation within the human species. Of the seven-plus billion on our planet, no two humans are alike. Let's take a closer look at some of the exceptional students and what's really different for them.

ACADEMICALLY CHALLENGED STUDENTS

Many students you work with are struggling. Some of the most common challenges are academic and behavioral underperformance. Teachers commonly think of IQ as being fixed, but it is not and can be changed (Nesbitt, 2009). Generally, there is strong heritability (80 percent or more) for general intelligence as measured by IQ test performance (Bouchard, 2009). But IQ is most heritable when the child was born into an upper- or middle-class family. That's because better health, access to opportunity, and fewer risk factors can allow for greater heritability. The heritability of parental IQ among children who grow up poor is below 10 percent (Tucker-Drob, Rhemtulla, Harden, Turkheimer, & Fask, 2011; Turkheimer, Haley, Waldron, D'Onofrio, & Gottesman, 2003).

In short, for kids who grow up in poverty, environmental factors are more likely than genes to adversely contribute to their basic intelligence as measured by IQ. This is a reminder: regardless of parental IQ, kids who are underperforming academically can improve. Many other factors will influence how he or she turns out. The question is, Can you apply the positive factors, such as effort building, cognitive capacity enhancing, or attitude building, that we learned in earlier chapters quickly so that the student can have a fighting chance to succeed in life?

One way to think about your students is to consider that it only takes a "threshold" of positive factors for them to succeed. Students don't need to be perfect or even great to succeed—but they do need the essentials. Your student's brain has overlapping, specialized operating systems (which are an aggregate of skills, habits, and attitudes), including a social one, an academic one, and a private one. Even young children have various operating systems, but theirs are quite raw and undeveloped, depending on their age and life experiences.

Here's a way to understand the operating system concept. The earliest computers had so little processing power that no matter how slowly you typed, you still tended to overwhelm the system. If you want to work fast at your computer today, you need fast chip processing and a large working memory (RAM). Now, fast-forward to your current day at work. Raising standards and having high expectations are admirable, but you've got to "enable" and build the brain's operating systems to make progress happen. Whatever you've done in the past with a student that worked, in effect it "upgraded" that student's operating system. Every successful school intervention for kids from low-income families features a variation on the theme of upgrading the operating system, a process that involves concentrating on the "fewest processes that matter most" to the learning process. But if you simply try to cram more content into the same brain without upgrading the operating system, the student will get bored, frustrated, or both, and will be likely to fail. To "make it" in school, the student needs a strong academic operating system. These are the critically needed, "home-run" skill areas:

- Attention and focus
- Self-control and deferred gratification
- Working memory
- Sequencing and prioritization
- Effort
- Attitude and the growth mind-set

The good news is that skills in every one of these areas are teachable. We've shown you how to strengthen those skills in the last few chapters. But for students who struggle, the brain is often overwhelmed by risk factors for academic or social impairment—poverty, parental separation, abuse, neglect, poor nutrition, bullying, lack of housing stability, and health issues. What teachers see on a behavioral level could range from mild attention deficit/hyperactivity disorder (ADHD) to severe conduct disorder. On an academic level, what they see might vary from treatable dyslexia to severe autism. You can't change the risk factors very easily, but you can strengthen the brain's social and academic operating systems as a counterforce.

Because of the potential impact of a targeted approach, whereby you narrow your focus and develop specific "high-yield" skills, such as visual working memory, students are not stuck the way they are. Their success is dependent on building capacity in regard to operating systems—and on its being upgraded. For example, we showed in Chapter Four that skills pertaining to attention, processing, and working memory can be built. To put it bluntly, building capacity to learn (upgrading executive function) *is much more important* than adding more content. Consider whether you tend to focus on building capacity or on adding content—and understand that you, as a caring, savvy teacher, have a pivotal role in upgrading students' academic or behavioral operating system, which is essential if students are to learn and process the academic information you wish to impart.

Here, we'll provide the foundation. When you see kids struggle, be sure to initiate these success strategies:

WHAT YOU CAN DO

- Build and strengthen your relationships with your struggling students. Find out what interests them, what motivates them, and what their concerns and stressors are. Build trust by being reliable, honest, and discreet (never share any information about a student with another student).

- Tell your students that as long as they do their part, you won't let them fail. Tell them that you are their partner and ally in the learning process. Remind them that you'll do everything you know how to help them—they just have to meet you halfway.

- Remind students that brains can and do change. Tell them brains are malleable—all they need to do is follow the teacher's rules, assignments, and guidelines for change (discussed in Chapter Two). Be clear about this fundamental point: kids are not stuck the way they are. Optimism is critical.

ACADEMICALLY GIFTED STUDENTS

Being gifted and talented suggests having either a high level of general intelligence or having a domain-specific ability, such as musical talent (Kalbfleisch, 2004). What more recent research suggests is that what is commonly called "talent" is actually not some mysterious and innate "gift." We have all seen early hints of talent or near genius that never seemed to develop. For a learner with certain traits to emerge as a full-blown, exceptionally bright student, it takes the following factors (Colvin, 2008):

- Deliberate practice specifically designed to improve task performance
- High repetition
- Actionable feedback on results
- A mentor or source of advice
- Passion toward the goal

Teachers who help students arrange those five factors will see these learners develop into strong achievers (rather than stagnate).

Although researchers can find differences in the brains of those who are more typical students versus those who have been identified as gifted, it is the life experiences that create the biggest differences. Similarly, the brain differences that have shown up are both early and measurable. Here are a few of them:

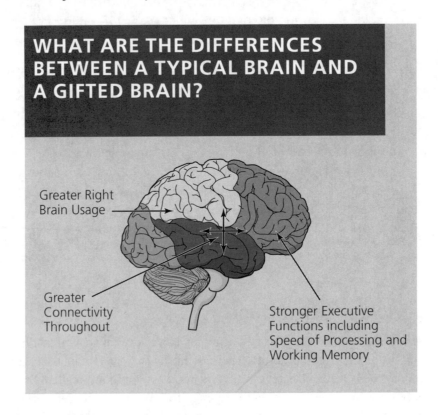

WHAT ARE THE DIFFERENCES BETWEEN A TYPICAL BRAIN AND A GIFTED BRAIN?

Greater Right Brain Usage

Greater Connectivity Throughout

Stronger Executive Functions including Speed of Processing and Working Memory

> **In most gifted students, we see the following:**
>
> - **Greater executive function (frontal lobes)**
> - **More right brain use**
> - **More consistent alpha wave brain patterns**
> - **Greater brain connectivity: front to back and side to side**
> - **More productive brain chemistry that can enhance learning**
> - **Better working memory for juggling and processing thoughts**

Some have observed that gifted children are often beset with social and emotional difficulties that make their life miserable, with frustration in school, difficulty finding like-minded friends, and social angst (Winner, 2000). This has some truth to it; but it's also true that many students with certain learning disabilities also have a higher likelihood of social and emotional problems (Semrud-Clikeman, Walkowiak, Wilkinson, & Minne, 2010; St. Clair, Pickles, Durkin, & Conti-Ramsden, 2011). This suggests that some of the problems may stem from brain differences—or they may be a result of the students' being labeled as "different," which can start a chain reaction of changed perceptions leading to changed behaviors.

There's no doubt that children in either the top or the bottom 3 percent of any population in terms of IQ are very different in mental functioning and behaviors. Many minorities are underrepresented in the gifted population, especially those living in poverty (Duncan & Magnuson, 2005). Research indicates that compared to their representation in the population at large, the proportion of blacks and Hispanics identified as gifted is only half of that expected (the percentage of the general population versus the percentage identified as gifted: African Americans—16 percent versus 8 percent; Hispanics—9 percent versus 4.7 percent) (Chan and Kitano, 1986). This suggests the importance of having a very open mind when it comes to what giftedness looks and sounds like. Is there a quick, "teacher-friendly" way to detect the traits of giftedness? No single profile can describe all the gifted students, but these students do share some strong common tendencies. Following are the five personality traits or qualities most consistent with giftedness and strategies you can use to work with them:

WHAT TO WATCH FOR

- Gifted students want to "get it right" and dislike sloppy work (perfectionism). This also means they can be very critical of themselves. You'll need help them develop "thinking rubrics" to evaluate their own work more effectively. For example, include speed, efficiency, and clear standards as criteria for self-evaluation (95 percent accuracy, not 100 percent, is acceptable if it's great quality and it works).

- Gifted students are constantly attracted to novelty and creative ways to see, hear, and do things (*creativity*). You'll need to have them develop their own rubric, which may or may not include divergent ideas, so that they have a guideline with which to judge when creativity is valuable and when it is "fool's gold."

- Gifted students can be emotionally intense, and often have a greater moral, ethical, and social awareness of the world and its dangers (*sensitivity*). You'll want to be sure to invest a bit of extra time (1) checking in with them daily, and (2) teaching them how to reframe personal and social problems in ways that make sense to them. Also, be sure to include guiding them on how to deal with stressors they can't control.

- Gifted students have an ability to focus on a task relentlessly (*intensity*). They can be high achievers because they're willing to put in the effort. Help them see, and reinforce often, that effort is only one of the success drivers (effort, attitude, focused strategy, and cognitive capacity). When students over-rely on effort alone, it can make them inefficient (sometimes a change of strategy is better) and unhappy.

- Gifted students often look at things in ways that are far different from how the typical student views them (*being different*). This can be both a blessing and a curse. You'll want to give students opportunities to express their insights in class, such as by doing a weekly comic strip, writing short essays and op-ed pieces, or drawing so that others can see their views in a way that is "approved."

Source: Adapted from the National Society for the Gifted & Talented, 2012.

EXPANDED KEY SKILLS

- **Self-control:** the capacity to restrain impulsivity and the ability to defer gratification. This is particularly difficult for those with ADHD and gifted learners, both of whom can get impatient.

- **Effort:** long-term motivation. For the gifted, the project has to be challenging and complex. For those with disabilities, it takes a far greater system of academic, social, and emotional support.

- **Attentional skills:** the ability to engage, focus, and disengage as needed. These must be upgraded in those with ADHD.

- **Organizing:** prioritizing tasks. This is a key skill that should be taught to all students.

- **Memory capacity:** short-term and working memory. Those with attention deficit disorder or ADHD typically have poor working memory.

- **Sequencing skills:** knowing the order of steps in a process. Kids with learning difficulties often struggle with this and need skill building.

- **Processing skills:** auditory, visual, and tactile. These skills are commonly lacking in kids with learning delays and dyslexia.

- **Vocabulary.** Gifted kids often have a much stronger vocabulary, whereas those with learning disabilities often lack a grade-level vocabulary.

Many gifted children have some type of learning disability (Lovett & Sparks, 2011). Both the disability and the giftedness often go undetected because giftedness can hide disabilities and disabilities depress IQ scores or talent indicators. Some children with disabilities are able to use strong abstract reasoning to adjust their learning strategies and compensate for weaknesses, making their disabilities that much harder for others to uncover. In today's schools, being gifted can be a disadvantage. For a child who already knows the material being presented to the class but has no choice but to sit through the lesson, the day stretches out unbearably—and no learning whatsoever takes place. Quality education, after all, works by a simple principle: contrast. If there is no difference between what you already know and what is offered, there is no contrast, and therefore no new learning.

Many high achievers in our society, including comedian Chris Rock, were high school dropouts who thought school made no sense for them. Jan and Bob Davidson, authors of *Genius Denied* (2004), say that up to 20 percent of dropouts are ''gifted,'' but they quit school because they felt ignored and unchallenged, bored and frustrated. As the Davidsons point out, if you taught the alphabet every day to senior high school students, not only would they learn nothing and be insulted but also over time they would lose ground by not getting the challenges they need to stay in school. That's what gifted students are up against.

WHAT YOU CAN DO

- Drop the use of labels (''You are so smart'' is a big mistake) with students, staff, and parents. Instead focus on effort, strategy, and attitude—all of which are within a student's control. Being labeled as ''smart'' can prompt some to try less (no need to work hard) or even to cheat to keep up appearances of high intelligence.

- No surprises when you pre-assess: give your students the ''end-of-semester final exam'' *at the start of the semester* to find out what students really know in advance. Use that as a working document to help guide strength building.

- Offer gifted students the option of completing an independent project on the topic you are teaching or allow them to substitute another experience of their choosing that would meet the objectives of the assignment (such as taking a college course).

- Explore acceleration possibilities. You may want to allow learners to attend classes with students who are at the same developmental level, rather than with peers in their age group. If a junior in high school can demonstrate that he is ready to learn university-level math, why should he be forced to take a lower-level math class just because of his age?

- Make it a priority to praise student effort rather than just the finished product.

- Mistakes are fine, but only if the student learns from them. Stop to help students debrief mistakes they have made to better understand what happened.

- Nurture students' interests with verbal encouragement and by helping them locate resources of greater complexity and meaning.

- Involve parents as resource locators and ensure that they are allies. Parents should be active advocates for their children.

- Discover distance learning opportunities. The choices for those looking for support are far greater than ever before thanks to the Web. Look for advanced placement math, science, and arts tutorials. The online video series put out by www.ted.com/talks can provide powerful inspiration.

Many well-meaning educators make common mistakes when working with gifted learners. First, stop making assumptions about these learners, and start asking more questions. Second, avoid asking them to be tutors for struggling students. Gifted children typically think and learn differently than other students, and asking them to serve as tutors can be a frustrating experience for all parties involved. Third, do not put the gifted students in the same lockstep process as other students. If they can pass a competency exam, consider grade-level or subject-level acceleration. Finally, it is common practice to give gifted students more work if they complete their assignments early. This is silly; provide them with higher, more complex and meaningful levels of work, not more of the same. A good resource is online at www.davidsongifted.org/db/Articles_id_10075.aspx.

Your understanding of what's going on in the brains of gifted learners is critical. They are not just kids who need to be kept busy; they need you to understand and appreciate how they are different and modify your instruction and curriculum. With a modified approach, you can expect better results. With that in mind, let's revisit the student at the beginning of the chapter.

Remember Jason from the beginning of the chapter? Jason was fortunate; in fact, you could say he hit the ''academic lottery.'' He just happened to have a teacher who saw his differences as unique factors, not ''issues.'' Instead of telling him about how he was not reaching his potential, his teacher focused on what he already did well. Affirmations and guidance worked. Instead of getting frustrated, the teacher looked for small pieces of the puzzle that could make the difference. Jason seemed to have several things going on. His executive function skills were low (skill building changed academic results), and he needed someone who believed in him (relationships). With a steady hand, encouragement, and some new ''learn to learn'' skills, Jason looks like he'll be making it this year. He's not yet an A student, but he's starting to believe in himself, and that's the first step.

TO SUM UP

We opened the chapter with Jason, a student who was struggling. The truth is, it took a special teacher to recognize why he was struggling and to design a successful intervention. There is no fixed destiny for struggling students; when you see one who is ''losing'' the battle in school, stop and ask questions. ''Is this an effort problem? Or is this a cognitive difficulty? Or is it an 'attitude problem' to work on?'' Every one of these challenges can be mitigated with strong teaching. With each of the challenges facing different learners, there's a different balance of what's needed to maximize the change in the brain. In every case, building relationships is critical. Without the connection, there is little chance of success. In some cases, building hope is vital. In others, skill building will solve most of the problems a student is experiencing. The real take-home messages here are that (1) differences are the norm, (2) differences mean you have to be different, (3) differences do not necessarily mean disabilities, (4) you can help every student succeed if you learn to use the right perspective in understanding and supporting each one.

Student Handout: Know and Strengthen Unique Abilities

- **Recognize your uniqueness as a student.** *Every student in your class has a different kind of brain from every other student. And every one of those brains functions in a slightly different manner. All students have both strengths and weaknesses. Know what your strengths are, build on them, and have the courage to identify and work on your weaknesses.*

- **Ask for help tailored to your own abilities and skills.** *Part of knowing how to ask for help is knowing what kinds of activities work for you as a student and which don't. For example, some students process information best through listening, whereas others need graphic representations to understand concepts. Think about how you learn best and share this information with your teachers.*

- **Manage your boredom.** *It is all too easy to assume that if you're bored it's the teacher's fault, or that school itself is simply boring. Human beings are learning machines. We naturally find learning new things interesting. There's usually something of interest in even the most boring of academic tasks. Focus on the interesting elements. Get into the habit of thinking that you are responsible for your own boredom. Don't blame the teacher!*

- **Recognize that human brains do develop and grow.** *You may have heard that the brain stops growing and developing at about eighteen years of age (that's false). Or that you have the most brain cells you will ever have when you are born, and that they start dying off at that point, never to be replaced (that's false). New insights about the brain have rendered statements like these obsolete. Your body does make new brain cells, and, even more important, whenever you learn to do something new, your brain builds important new connections.*

- **Let your creativity shine through.** *One of the great things about having so many different kinds of brains in the same classroom is that different brains mean fresh approaches. You may be sitting in the classroom listening to the teacher describe how to do a math problem, for example, when you have a flash of insight. You can do the problem in a different way! Share your insight. There are usually many different ways to tackle a single task.*

CHAPTER SEVEN

STRENGTHEN BODY, MIND, AND SOUL

Gary was having a miserable year in school. He was blamed by his teacher for many things he didn't do, such as stealing from classmates, cheating on tests, and starting fights. No one seemed to like him, and his mother was called to school frequently for disciplinary concerns. His mother wondered what had happened to her precious son who was a joy to the entire family, the son who had done well in school up until then. It was as if he had turned into a different person when he entered the school doors for fourth grade. All the issues at school made life at home difficult as well. Gary got sick more often, seemed depressed, and would do almost anything to avoid going to school. The exasperating year finally came to an end, and everyone who knew Gary breathed a sigh of relief.

The next school year rolled around all too quickly, met with much apprehension. Gary's mother tried to motivate him with talks about doing his best and how this was a new year, but was just as troubled as Gary was about another year of school. A strange thing began to happen as the new school year unfolded, however. Gary did his homework, got up on time, and was rarely sick. His mother received few calls from school, and the first report card showed a vast improvement in grades. What could have happened to facilitate this dramatic change? As his mother talked to Gary, the truth slowly came out. Last year's teacher seemed not to like Gary; in fact, it appeared the teacher would have done anything to avoid having Gary in class. In sharp contrast to last year's teacher, the current teacher loved Gary and thought he was one of the neatest kids she had ever taught. Gary's feeling of rejection by his previous teacher had had a negative impact on Gary's entire being—his body, mind, and soul. Although this story pertains to grades four and five, the message is the same for all grade levels. Good relationships matter. There is no age at which relationships cease to be important, and this is especially true with a struggling teenager.

The mother in this story is one of the authors of this book, and this experience became the deciding factor in Carole's completing her degree in education and embarking on a lifelong career of making a positive difference in the lives of young people. The body, mind, and soul are intricately connected, with a change in one area triggering changes in the others. In Gary's case, when his soul was negatively influenced, he experienced negative changes in his body and mind. In this chapter we will examine each area separately while recognizing the synergistic connection between the three.

BODY

As a teacher, your goal is to feed the students' minds, to help them grow intellectually. To meet this goal it is imperative to recognize the impact that the body has on learning and how you can influence this in a positive way. Oftentimes it is forgotten that the brain is indeed a physical part of the body and needs proper hydration, food, exercise, and rest. Students' physical condition can have a major impact on learning.

Hydration

"Water, water everywhere, nor any drop to drink," taken from *The Rime of the Ancient Mariner*, is a quote known by many. Today for most of your students you could say, "Water, water everywhere, and no one drinks a drop." Adequate hydration can improve both memory and attention (Benton, 2011). The operative word from this research is "adequate." Many students drink excessive amounts of caffeine in the form of colas, energy drinks, and coffee, all of which act as natural diuretics, keeping in mind that diuretics reduce the body's water volume by increasing the kidney's urine production (Kleiner, 1999). These drinks seem more appealing due to a combination of acquired taste, advertising, and the belief that any liquid will fulfill the body's need for adequate hydration. In reality, this need is best fulfilled by water, not by any of the other tempting substitutes (Kleiner, 2004). The implementation gap between hydration knowledge and application of this knowledge is huge, with immense negative results for students.

Bodies have a high need for water (Jequier & Constant, 2010). How much do your students actually require? The answer is based on many factors, including age, gender, weight, activity level, and environment. The traditional eight glasses of water a day is outdated and should be replaced with a more individualized approach. On average, an inactive male needs twelve cups of water per day, and an inactive female needs nine cups of water per day, with these numbers being adjusted upward as activity increases (Kleiner, 2004). For students who are not maintaining adequate hydration, setting a hydration goal, starting slowly, and sipping water throughout the day will result in the desired outcome of a well-hydrated brain. Dehydrated students will demonstrate a degree of impaired cognitive ability, such as lessened short-term memory functioning (Cian, Barraud, Melin, & Raphel, 2001). Because effective use of short-term memory is essential for ease of learning, a well-hydrated brain is an excellent learning aid. In your classroom and school setting, it's time for changes.

WHAT YOU CAN DO

- Share the importance of having a well-hydrated brain to enhance memory and attention.
- Permit water bottles in the classroom.
- Model drinking water rather than coffee and cola drinks in your classroom.

Nutrition

What your students eat matters greatly! Even though there is not one food that could be labeled as a "miracle food," it is important to recognize that some foods are much healthier than others. By the teenage years, habits are ingrained, and many students are sitting in their early morning classes fortified with nothing more than a quick energy drink. They feel good because they chose the sugarless form and have no idea they are decreasing their brain's optimum functioning. Addressing the connection between brain function and diet is often overlooked as a tool to promote ease of learning. The brain needs a steady flow of glucose for optimum functioning, and eating a variety of healthy foods three to five times a day will facilitate this. Lean protein combined with complex carbohydrates in the morning can provide the needed brain fuel for a great morning of learning. Lean protein also is effective in improving glycemic control, helping regulate the amount of sugar in the blood (Wycherley et al., 2010). Given the excessive amounts of sugar consumed by many students, how to obtain glucose through healthier eating becomes essential knowledge for current and long-range health.

Even with all the information about healthy eating, diets still tend to be high in fat and sugar, coupled with an absence of the needed lean protein and fresh fruits and vegetables. One of the primary reasons for this imbalance is that fast food is often cheaper and more easily obtained than healthier choices (Khan, Powell, & Wada, 2012). Although it is generally accepted by students that healthy eating is a good thing, changing eating habits can be overwhelming. Trying to change too quickly through fad dieting or eliminating all sugar and junk food is the radical road to food failure. As with hydration, a slower, more thoughtful approach can produce the desired results of improved eating habits.

Breakfast food choices, what one eats for breakfast, matter so much that they even affect the amount of gray matter in the brain (Taki et al., 2010). Reared in a world of instant gratification, teenagers are more interested in fast results from dietary changes than eating healthy for the long haul. A goal of improved brain function bears little resemblance to a goal of dropping two sizes by the prom. The good news is that both goals—improving brain function and achieving a healthier weight—can be obtained by identifying and adhering to a more healthful diet. Eating for health and improved brain function rather than fad dieting for quick weight loss will facilitate a natural loss of weight while optimizing brain function. This is not an easily assumed task in a society prone to the consumption of fast food loaded with fat and offering little nutrition. Limiting access to fast food and consistently emphasizing daily good choices when it comes to eating form the pathway to better health and brain function. It may seem that educators have limited influence on their students when it comes to diet, but there are actually many ways teachers can promote healthy eating.

EAT THE RAINBOW

Include as many different colors of food in your diet as possible.

WHAT YOU CAN DO

- Campaign to ensure the school's food menus are healthy.

- Avoid using junk food or candy as a reward.

- Share your healthy food choices and your reasons for them.

- Teach students to take baby steps on the pathway to healthy eating. For example, suggest that they could replace one junk food with a healthier choice weekly or biweekly.

- Reinforce that food choices can support or undermine brain function.

Exercise

The benefits of exercise appear to be boundless. Your students will feel better, behave more appropriately, and have enhanced cognitive function. Physical activity can even play an important role in reducing depressive symptoms (Paluska & Schwenk, 2000). Yet the term *couch potato* applies to a great number of students. The electronic age has helped entrench the sedentary lifestyle in our society. Further, an era of testing and budget cuts has many schools eliminating recess and physical education in the name of raising student achievement.

A quick review of the research supports the assertion that exercise has a positive influence on brain function (Ratey & Loehr, 2011). The classroom does not have to become a gym, but using movement to review, refocus, or provide a quick break will reap untold benefits. For a quick review, divide students into small groups and have them toss a ball to each other to answer review questions provided by you. Students grasp and retain more information through movement (implicit learning) than through the more traditional lecture approach (explicit learning). A great method to teach the sequence of historical events is to place the events on index cards and have students position themselves in correct historical order using the cards. A student's brain abounds in complexity, and exercise is a tool that is well documented to improve learning (Cotman & Berchtold, 2002). The study by Cotman and Berchtold showed that exercise improved brain plasticity, which leads to enhanced learning.

Through fun and positive classroom movement, students can become more aware of their exercise patterns outside of the classroom, facilitating their realization that exercise improves fitness, increases one's energy level, and aids in managing stress (Kannangara et al., 2011). Sustained aerobic exercise will also increase the size of the anterior hippocampus in the brain, which leads to improvements in memory (Erickson et al., 2011). Developing the exercise habit as a teenager can lead to a lifetime of healthy movement. The person who continues to strive for fitness as he or she ages can maintain hippocampal function, ward off depression, and sustain memory function (Erickson, Miller, & Roecklein, 2012).

Eliminating physical education is easy to accomplish because many states have weak or no requirements in this area. This is not justification for eliminating it, but it does provide us with an understanding of why it is happening in so many districts. Armed with the knowledge of how critical exercise is for supporting and promoting academic function, begin to learn your state's basic standards in this area. Keeping the classroom energized and filled with engaging, fun, and stimulating activities is a great starting place for taking into account the importance of physical activities to enhance learning.

WHAT YOU CAN DO

- Assign student-led teams to facilitate energizers in each of your classes, so that role is handled by the kids rather than by you. Add such movement as stretches, touching three different walls for a quick break, and ball tosses led by you or the students for review. Your kids will love it.

- Bump up the classroom activity level. Add "walk and talk" activities, with students each walking and talking with a peer to discuss newly learned material.

- Encourage kids to play sports of any kind; they can do this at a YMCA, Boys & Girls Club, or elsewhere.

Sleep

The amount of sleep teenagers need can vary, but the bottom line is that sleep deprivation is common in this group. Middle schools and high schools usually have the earliest start times, and many teenagers typically go to bed too late to get an adequate night's rest. Students from low-income families, large families, and minority groups tend to go to bed later (Blair et al., 2012), and when these students have to rise at a set hour for school, sleep deprivation often results. Most students know they feel much better after a good night's sleep but have limited understanding of sleep's benefits for the brain. Adequate sleep plays a critical role in memory consolidation; inadequate sleep results in distractibility and inattention for students (Carskadon, 2011). Sleep deprivation has a negative impact on the prefrontal cortex (Leenaars et al., 2012), which regulates the executive function skills needed for academic success.

Ensuring Adequate Sleep

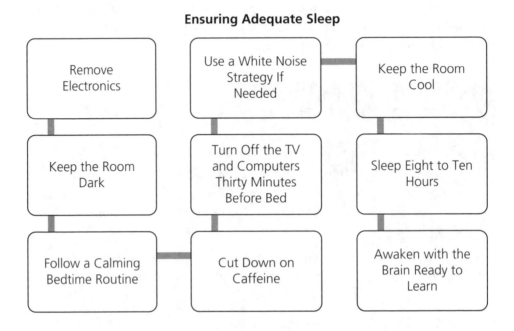

Here's the key take-home message:

WHAT YOU CAN DO

- Remind students to get needed sleep (seven-plus hours every night). Encourage students to turn off all electronics at least thirty minutes before going to bed.

- Do not allow kids to sleep in class; it will become a habit. Make every minute of class count.

- Share the value of bedtime routines for all weeknights. For students who need a steady, rhythmic sound to sleep well, encourage them to use any white noise strategy, such as running a fan.

Even though it is not part of your job description, remember you may be the only adult promoting a healthy lifestyle to enhance student learning. This is time well spent by you.

MIND

A student's mind is so active, focused on content of his or her own choosing, while school subjects are often afforded minimal time and effort. Why? The young mind yearns for novelty, challenge, and complexity, coupled with periods of revitalization; and whether or not the student believes it, the mind thrives on new learning. The secret is for the student to learn to self-regulate so that his or her mind does what he or she wants it to do.

This self-regulation can be accomplished with inspirational reading; avoiding negative thoughts and lyrics; spending time with quality, uplifting company; and focusing on things that bring personal joy. Most middle and high school students spend huge amounts of time using Facebook and Twitter, texting, and hanging out with friends rather than doing homework or seeking more mind-stimulating activities. These activities aren't necessarily bad, but they can consume immense amounts of time that could be used to hone the mind to razor-sharpness rather than allowing it to become dull with a lack of stimulation. There are many challenging game and activity websites, such as www.lumosity.com, designed to do just this. These websites are not age specific, and they offer increasing degrees of complexity for continual challenge. These activities can be very appealing to a generation of students with sophisticated high-tech skills.

Reintroduce kids to board games and puzzles, take them on trips to new places, and direct them to mind-stimulating Internet websites. Also remember that many struggling students do not have ready access to more costly options for mind improvement, such as visiting theaters, museums, or even the library, due to financial and transportation issues. Consider examining ways to make these options more available to students if possible. Parent organizations, community agencies, or local businesses often can provide the needed monies or transportation for students. We are both big fans of teaching students mindfulness skills. Students' personal awareness of what they are doing with their mind is of paramount importance. Teach mindfulness through such activities as these four:

- **Being in the present moment**. Teach kids to be ''right here'' now. When you are fully present, you can feel the joy of the moment. There is NO guilt from your past or anxiety about the future. Here kids learn to pay attention to what they are experiencing in the present moment.

- **Practicing awareness**. Teach your kids to pay attention to just one sense at a time, and enjoy it. Then rotate to a new sense. Use all five senses to notice background sights, sounds, smells, sensations, textures, colors, and light.

Next, practice awareness of the senses by asking students to contribute dialogue or opinions concerning each sense.

- **Using a beginner's mind.** This is a learning activity that frees students from the prejudice of prior learning. Say to students, ''Imagine you are a child, experiencing an activity for the first time. You have never experienced this before, and you don't know what to expect. You are excited and curious.'' Ask students to pause and write a paragraph about this ''beginner's mind'' experience.

- **Avoiding judgment.** Teach students to observe internal and external events without judging them or labeling them (''That sucks!''). Show them how to observe these events, and how to respond with compassion and understanding. For example, ''He didn't call me like he said he would. So I think I'll call him instead to make sure everything is okay.''

Remember, many of the students who are ''hardest to reach'' have been cast aside by family, friends, and society. They cannot afford to have you give up on them too. When you give up on them, they will most certainly give up on themselves.

WHAT YOU CAN DO

- Promote attendance at free cultural events or school-sponsored enrichment activities.

- Introduce students to websites for mind stimulation, such as junglememory.com or www.lumosity.com.

- Teach mindfulness skills, such as reflection, expressing gratitude, and focusing. Use some of the mindfulness activities listed earlier.

SOUL

Every student is uniquely who he or she is for many reasons. Genetics and environment have each contributed to make this teenager who sits in front of you daily. The student is a whole human being—body, mind, and soul. Each of the three components is constantly interacting with the others; and each needs to be fully developed if the whole person is to achieve maximum functioning. As we examine the last of the three, the soul, let's begin by defining it. It is that innermost being that could also be described as one's spirit. As with the body and mind, the spirit thrives on good nourishment, the substances that make it better, the substances that feed it. You are in the very unique position of being able to teach students ways to feed their spirit. This teaching is a beautiful example of implicit instruction at its finest. Students will watch, internalize, and respond to all you say and do in the classroom. Here, we'll introduce three ways to feed the soul: quality relationships, reflection, and community service.

Relationships

Respect and acceptance feed the soul. When you greet students at the door, call them by name, and exhibit an interest in each of them as a person, you will indeed be a soul feeder. Good relationships and social acceptance rank high in soul building. Students with limited acceptance by others often see life as less meaningful (Stillman et al., 2009), which can have a deleterious impact on their desire to learn. Limited acceptance is seen too often in our schools today. These are the kids who have few friends, experience frequent feelings of loneliness, and know they will never be a part of any "in-group." As you continue to build positive teacher-student relationships, remember that these relationships can enhance students' academic success. Good teacher-student relationships constitute one of the greatest predictors of academic success, and the relationships built as early as kindergarten can be a predictive factor for test scores, grades, and disciplinary outcomes in later years (Hamre & Pianta, 2001). Students will also be quick to sense when teachers have positive relationships with other staff members. That teenage radar is alive and well, and students benefit from the modeling of positive adult relationships. Just like at home, if they can divide and conquer, they certainly will. Keeping staff relationships positive eliminates the opportunity for them to do this, and provides students with a sense of hope when adults work together for students' benefit.

Reflection

For many teens, journal writing is a wonderful opportunity to express emotions in a safe way. Positive journal writing, such as in a gratitude journal, can be very beneficial to students. With many teens focusing on what they are not and what they do not have, the powerful attitude of gratitude totally eludes them. Writing can help them think about, focus on, and listen to their own feelings. Emotions are powerful and will always have an impact on learning. On the one hand, memory is enhanced by emotional events. We tend to remember such events as weddings, birthdays, or holidays due to the positive emotional attachment. On the other hand, emotions that distract from the focus on learning, such as anger or depression, will have a negative impact on working memory (Wong et al., 2012). Emotions and cognition have a high correlation for all students. Keeping them engaged in the writing process gives them a way to feed their soul in a reflective way. Many teens struggle with negative emotions, such as feelings of inferiority, jealousy, and helplessness (Seligman, Rashid, & Parks, 2006). They will need your guidance as they create gratitude journals—and by incorporating this writing into your class, you will be able to provide the needed support.

Community Service

Community service can feed the souls of the volunteer as well as the recipients of services. As much as possible, let students choose service projects that reflect their interests and that will be meaningful to them. This will ensure a higher rate of quality volunteering (Seaman, 2012) and provide a reduction in levels of alienation coupled with improved school behavior (Calabrese & Schumer, 1986). According to Calabrese and Schumer, community service developed responsibility in students and created an environment of collaboration and cooperation. Assuming responsibility and being more willing to work collaboratively and cooperatively with others led to the improved school behavior. Students quickly discover that by helping others, they in turn are helping themselves as well. Serving others feeds the soul.

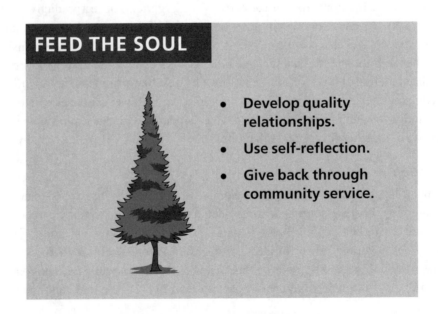

FEED THE SOUL

- **Develop quality relationships.**
- **Use self-reflection.**
- **Give back through community service.**

WHAT YOU CAN DO

- Strengthen your relationships with your students and assist them in forming positive relationships with each other through classroom activities and teamwork. Ensure your classroom is a safe, enriching place to be, with many types of learning opportunities, so that kids just want to be in your room.

- Allow students to connect and reflect through both structured and unstructured writing activities. Reflection is a powerful tool for feeding the soul, and positive emotions and gratitude provide all of us with nourishment.

- Make community service easy for kids to get into. Start with a class project that everyone does together; then open up the options for students to continue on their own with other projects in the community.

TO SUM UP

The body, mind, and soul are inextricably linked, with each always having an impact on the other two. For you as a teacher, it is so easy to get lost in the daily routines of enhancing each student's mind that you may give little thoughtful attention to feeding the soul or building the body. Searching out ways to reach the physical and spiritual sides of students will reap myriad benefits. Who doesn't want a student who is more caring, more thoughtful, or less angry? Wouldn't it be wonderful if all students were well rested, well fed, and ready to learn each day? Even though teaching focuses primarily on the mind, the wise teacher understands the importance of the body and spirit as well.

Every great achiever has put hours and hours into skill development. If one wants to perform at Carnegie Hall or compete in the Olympics, a great investment of time and effort is needed. Besides building a specific skill set, the performer or athlete devotes time and energy to the development of the whole person in the interest of dream achievement. The same is true for students in a classroom. If each student is to perform at his or her best, the total person needs to be addressed. Time spent pursuing the building of the body through movement and good nutrition as well as feeding the soul through the pursuit of dreams and the creation of positive emotions is invaluable. By helping students achieve maximum functioning of the body and soul, you will contribute to maximizing the mind's functioning as well.

Student Handout: Take Care of Your Body, and Your Mind Will Benefit

- **Make sure you are eating a brain-healthy diet**. *You are surrounded by lots of bad food choices. In fact, one could argue that much of the food that is available to you isn't food at all. To feed your body and brain, try to eat real food—fresh vegetables and fruits, meat and fish, and good fats like olive oil—and go light on the carbohydrates, chips, and fries.*

- **Stay hydrated**. *There are many kinds of drinks on the market now that contain ingredients that are not beneficial to brain health and brain function. Avoid these and drink plain water instead. (It's free!) In particular, avoid drinks with caffeine.*

- **Exercise at least three times a week**. *Exercise isn't just important for a strong body, it's important for a strong brain as well! In fact, some exercise—such as activities in which you have to move laterally or remember complex steps—not only brings more blood and oxygen to the brain but also helps strengthen connections between different parts of the brain.*

- **Get a lot of sleep**. *Always shoot for at least eight and up to ten hours of sleep every night. When thinking about your weekly schedule, also consider sleep time. Many students think of the late-night hours as the time when they catch up on homework, but this is a mistake! Those hours are for sleeping, and research shows that during the adolescent years the body needs more sleep than during other times of life.*

- **Reduce "bad" stress**. *There are different kinds of stress. The brain and body respond well to good stressors—like creative challenges. Bad stress happens when you feel out of control. If you feel stressed, it may mean you are avoiding dealing with something important. Do that assignment that's been nagging at you. Talk to your teachers about your late work. Take charge. And don't forget to build in some time to relax.*

CHAPTER EIGHT

FOCUS STUDENTS ON GOALS

Sarah felt devastated. She'd gotten another D on her report card. Mom would be mad and yell again. Sarah hated her mom yelling at her and telling her she needed to get to work. She was busy all the time—how could she possibly do more? She kept up with her friends on Facebook, worked at her part-time job, took care of her pets, and tried to find time to do her homework. She took great pride in how well she juggled all these things. One day while contemplating her low grades and her mom's disappointment, she watched as her gerbil went round and round on its wheel. The proverbial light bulb went off in her head: Sarah felt like the gerbil on the wheel, keeping busy all the time but not really going anywhere. She knew at that very moment the reason for her low grades. She was spending all her time being busy, but not doing the things that really mattered.

This chapter examines how students can learn to set compelling goals that can lead to lifelong success. To catch a student's interest in goals today, you will need a fresh approach—something that will make goals more exciting, more alive. Most of your students will not have written down goals unless they were required to do so in class. Let's identify how to get your students to achieve Sarah's frame of mind—doing the things that have to be done first. By the way, Sarah started writing down what needed to be done each day and realized that she was setting goals. She really wanted to raise the D to a B. She was shocked because she had never liked writing goals before. Two things were very different this time, however, in that she had an intense *desire* to get a B, and she had an equally intense belief in the importance of her goal.

THE SKILLS OF ACHIEVING GOALS

Many students cannot clarify what it is they really want. A good starting point for you is helping students dream, think big, and make a wish list for their future. Many of them have thought jokingly about this, but have never gotten serious because they thought their dream was out of their reach. As their teacher, you understand that doing well in school can help them achieve whatever they really want in life. They do not. Remember this as you guide them through the main concepts of this chapter—learning to identify dreams, developing goals to match their dreams, and following the steps needed to achieve their dreams.

Yes, it is true that some people, throughout their lives, happen to be in the ''right place'' at the ''right time,'' and they move forward with a friend, a job, a stock tip, or a relationship. But although that does happen, relying on luck is a terrible lifelong strategy for becoming the person you dream about being. This chapter is all about how a person gets to where he or she wants to go. Although the chapter is written primarily with students in mind, this process might work best if you and your students start the year with dreams and work together to achieve them! Here's how the chapter will unfold.

DREAMS AND WISHES

Many of your students are so busy that they have never given any thought to what they really want and how doing well in school could help them get there. There is a vast difference between a student working hard for a purpose and a student working hard simply because that's what is expected. Academic and personal goals set at the beginning of a semester will serve as predictors of students' final grades (Zimmerman, Bandura, & Martinez-Pons, 1992). Students will be much more willing to set academic and personal goals when they have started by identifying their dreams. You have a dream as a teacher that they will do well in school and in their lives, and that they will pass enough of the mandated tests to keep everyone afloat. Your dreams and a student's personal dreams can mesh into a synergy that benefits all.

> **If your students don't seem to have any big dreams, introduce them to the world of big dreamers!**

Starting with students' dreams may be much larger than you had envisioned when initiating thinking about and teaching goal setting. However, it is only by starting with their individual dreams that many students will get excited and start to buy into the power of goals. The challenge for some of your students will be that they have no idea what they want. They have never peeked into their future with a long-range lens. They don't know what is available; they've never seen anything beyond their own world. Perhaps they will dream of owning an expensive car. Even that can be okay because possessing such a car is probably out of their range of current possibilities. They are setting their sights on something much larger than what they have at the present moment. All career possibilities, owning a pricey item, or even exotic travels are acceptable dreams; simply visualizing the attainment of any of these dreams will initiate a feeling of control and power for a student that can be a true asset. That feeling of power can lead them to prioritize their efforts to pursue their dreams effectively (DeWall, Baumeister, Mead, & Vohs, 2011). Your wisdom and understanding will be much needed as they start this dream quest. You will quickly ascertain that some dreams seem way too unrealistic, and yet it will be fun for you to see some of your students getting excited about their dreams. Build on this positive state to start the goal identification process.

Flow writing can be a wonderful way for students to begin their personal exploration. Have the students put "I want . . ." at the top of a piece of paper and just write for three minutes everything they want. Nothing is too big or too small. You will need to remind them to keep the lists positive and legal—students are not permitted to express dreams of hurting someone or of horrific events, for example. After they have written down their dreams, have students select one dream to pursue. Vague generalities need to be eliminated, such as "I just want to be happy" or "I want a good job." Students also need to own their dream and balance what others expect of them with what they really want for themselves.

This beginning activity can be very revealing for you. You will quickly note that this activity is out of some students' comfort zone. That is to be expected due to the novelty, but that same novelty can lead to engagement. This is the time when some learners will start to comprehend that they can choose their direction, their destination. The only thing they have to do is begin to actually start moving in the right direction. To reach a destination they must stay with it long enough to get there. This is a critical point. The road may be bumpy, they could run out of gas, or they may want to stop, but to reach their dream destination they must jump, stumble over, or get around each obstacle. You may need to check for appropriate destinations that are positive, and that do not require anything illegal. Once each student has chosen his or her dream, it is time to start the trip—with you as the guide. You can share with students that you will be teaching them the steps using the backwards goal design introduced later, to achieve their personal dream by guiding them through the process of goal setting. As the students begin identifying their dreams and wishes with their initial writing, remember to do the following:

WHAT YOU CAN DO

- Talk to students about their dreams. Most important, listen. Develop an accepting attitude in regard to their dreams. Try to use words or phrases to demonstrate your interest, such as "Fascinating," "Go for it!" "How long have you had this dream?" or "I see no reason why you couldn't do it."

- Be a role model. Talk about your own dreams, and what you did to become an educator (or to reach any other big goal). If students don't have dreams, just keep introducing them to big ideas. One of them will catch on.

- Take advantage of the Internet to open students' minds to hundreds of dreams. You may have many students who have no idea about the multitude of career choices available today. As their teacher, you want the best for your students, but you certainly don't have the time to do this extensive research for them (nor should you do it). Such sites as http://medicalcareerinfo .com or http://careersearch.com can lead to thousands of career choices for consideration.

GETTING STARTED ON GOALS

1. Identify a goal.

2. Write it down.

GOAL WRITING

So much has been written about setting goals, and so few people do it. Breaking down goal setting into small, manageable steps makes the process very doable. Starting with an exciting dream will inspire your students to want to begin, but they will need you to be their guide. Very few students can express their goals in writing on their own, especially your struggling students. Encouraging students to go after a dream can inspire and motivate them to action, whereas using the more traditional performance goals as a starting point can lead to inaction due to students' lack of passion for such basic performance goals. An emphasis on performance goals coupled with a student's having little confidence in his or her academic ability will result in a lack of committed, enthusiastic effort by the student (Elliott & Dweck, 1988). Students often internalize the belief that a performance goal is simply unobtainable and put forth minimal effort. Consistent lack of effort will always have a negative impact on academics—the total opposite of what you desire for your students. This is an essential difference between a focus on performance goals and the pursuit of a dream through a long-range goal.

Once students have selected their dream, you can have them substitute the word ''goal'' for ''dream,'' explaining that a clear dream is really a long-range goal. Now is a great time for the students to start a paper trail documenting the pursuit of their goal. You can decide if you want uniformity in their goal writing and consequent action steps by specifying a format for their writing, or you can let them choose how to record their journey. Usually struggling students will need specific directions from you.

The first step is for students to record their selected goal. There is great power in the recording of a goal. It starts to add urgency, coupled with clarity and focus. If a goal is not put on paper or an electronic device, the student may feel that he or she is doing nothing to accomplish the goal. Being willing to commit to a specific plan for a goal not only will aid in goal achievement but also will give students a sense of freedom to pursue other activities (Masicampo & Baumeister, 2011). The act of choosing and recording the goal is just the beginning, however. Developing and following goal attainment steps comes after goal selection.

WHAT YOU CAN DO

- Teach students the power of believing strongly in a goal. Does the goal represent what the student really wants, his or her dream? If it doesn't, the student will need to start over, making the goal personal and positive. If there is no passion for the goal, attainment is unlikely.

- Teach the skill of visualizing goal achievement. Students could each find or draw a picture representing their goal fulfilled and place it where they can view it daily. They could add words describing how they would feel if they were to achieve their goal, such as "proud," "powerful," and "successful."

- Determine, with students, their starting point. In the case of a large goal it's very easy for a student to procrastinate and not begin. You probably have seen this pattern in your students with any large project. Identifying the first small step facilitates action.

- Help students take their long-range goal and break it down. Students need to develop a plan using incremental steps to avoid feeling overwhelmed. A chart or mind map is a very useful tool to accomplish this, especially when starting with a long-range goal. Give students time to work on their goal weekly by using their self-developed chart for each step. The chart can eliminate procrastination due to an "I don't know what to do" mentality.

- Stay positive and celebrate. It could be years before a long-range career goal is actualized. This makes it imperative to have milestones set along the way, the attainment of which can be celebrated. For example, graduating from high school could be a major milestone in any student's pursuit of a long-range goal. When starting out, encourage students to celebrate every small victory to promote perseverance.

You can see that this approach is very different from some of the customary goal-setting formulas used by many today. Most of the current goal-setting formulas start with and focus exclusively on short-term goals. This approach tends to be teacher driven and fails to captivate the student's imagination and excitement. From such excitement, perseverance can be born. Perseverance is a characteristic that may be lacking in many of your struggling students, but it can be developed among students of any age and from any group. Perseverance is a form of resilience often found in individuals from low-income, urban groups who possess certain strengths needed to resist the adversity they face (Teti et al., 2012). The development of this kind of perseverance can imbue a life with the prospect of hope and success.

For teenagers living primarily in the here and now, your continued support will be essential for success in goal achievement. To sustain their steady progress, consider sharing some of your past goals and how you reached them, as well as your current goals. Identify some of the tools students have that may not have been available to you in achieving your earlier goals, such as iPhones or iPads. Electronic tools can replace the old paper-and-pencil method of goal setting and monitoring, and will be more readily embraced by tech-savvy teenagers. Frequent, informal check-ins convey the message that learners' goals are important and that you care. These check-ins can be handled much more expediently with the use of PDAs or tablets. Students will not be juggling paperwork and can quickly share their progress with you. The use of these tools will save classroom time and still keep students focused on long-term goal achievement.

FOSTERING THOUGHTFUL STRATEGIES

A long-range, dream-fulfilling goal is written knowing that attainment can take years. This could lull some students into believing that procrastination is okay. In reality, once the goal is determined and the work is initiated, the goal will determine behavior through the desire for goal attainment. This goal-driven behavior will eventually reach a level of positive automaticity for students (Dijksterhuis & Aarts, 2010). Fascinating, yes, but the key is to begin. Nothing will change; nothing will be gained without the initiation. Many of your students have become masters at never really beginning. They think about starting, talk about starting, but never start. You know this. The question is how to say to your class,

''Ladies and gentlemen, start your engines,'' so that everyone gets fired up and ready to go.

Procrastination is a widespread phenomenon in middle school and high school, and it often continues even into college. Because procrastination can have a negative impact on learning, achievement, academic self-efficacy, and quality of life (Rabin, Fogel, Nutter-Upham, 2011), this behavior among your students could require classroom interventions by you. Your classic procrastinators often need more than a verbal reminder to get started. They have become habituated to verbal warnings, resulting in their turning a deaf ear to them.

WHAT YOU CAN DO

- Show students how to make the first step toward their goal so small that it becomes almost impossible not to take it.

- Remind students to do just one small thing each day to keep them on track.

- Ask students to talk through what they are doing. Listen carefully for opportunities to affirm their effort, suggest a strategy, or offer some guidance.

Employing a backward design to achieve a goal can facilitate the needed action. Students simply need to start; when they don't, you will hear such statements as ''I don't know what to do'' or ''I don't get this goal stuff.'' The only way the initial work will be easy is if you have already walked students through a backward process. For example, if a student wants to be a medical doctor, the major milestones could seem overwhelming, resulting in procrastination. By working backward, the student moves from residency and internship to medical school, college, high school, current grade level, quarterly grades, weekly work, daily work, and immediate task. The immediate task then becomes a very focused, in-the-moment action. You can remind students that the only thing you are concerned about is the baby step needed for today. By taking daily baby steps, your students will make action a habit, and will begin working daily on their goal without constant reminders from you.

Backwards Goal Design

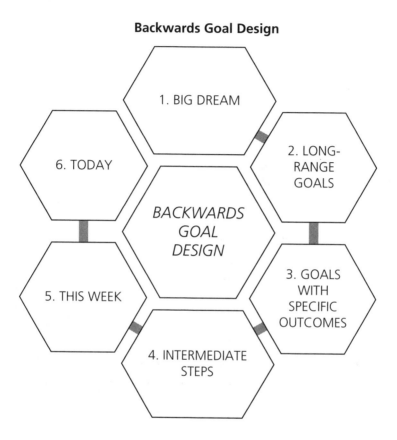

Another element that is key to goal attainment is giving goals priority time. Most students are busy doing something all the time. The problem is what they are choosing to do. It is tempting to participate in fun, engaging activities that have little to do with the chosen goal. Often these activities are worthwhile; they are just not the most important for goal attainment. Being able to postpone instant gratification and stick to the task at hand requires self-awareness and self-discipline. If goals are to be achieved, students must develop the self-discipline to say no to some leisure activities and persist in goal-directed behavior (Mischel, Shoda, & Rodriquez, 1989). Choosing goal achievement over leisure activities in this way is not an easy task for most students to accomplish. It will take time and practice, and will become easier each time self-discipline is chosen over self-indulgence.

Goal accomplishment takes an enormous time commitment, and yet everyone seems to lament the lack of time. Students are quick to pick up on this mind-set from parents, peers, and sometimes even their teachers. What is amazing is that when a student really wants to do something, such as shopping or keeping up with friends on Facebook, somehow it gets done. It once again becomes a matter of priorities and time management.

WHAT YOU CAN DO

- Kids need to learn what it takes to reach a goal. There are many activities for use in the classroom that take just a few minutes. Taking two minutes to update goal progress on an electronic device or checking goal-related websites are two examples that help students stay focused to achieve their goals. One of the sites to check out is www.youthwork -practice.com/games/cooperation-games.html.

- Share true stories of real people who overcame ridiculous odds to survive or to reach a goal. For example, Aron Ralston's memoir of the 127-hour incident, *Between a Rock and a Hard Place*, is gripping (as is the movie based on that story). While hiking alone in Blue John Canyon, Utah, Ralston's right arm was crushed and pinned by a falling boulder for 127 hours. It was only by self-amputation of his arm that he was able to free himself and get to help.

To overcome time obstacles, students need to make a true commitment to their goal. If students are to use their time effectively, they will have to want to reach the goal more than anything else. With this self-commitment in place, time management becomes a lesser issue. There always seems to be time to accomplish what really matters. Goals can foster the motivation needed to put in the long hours of work required for their achievement (Klein, Wesson, Hollenbeck, & Alge, 1999). Students can accomplish what they are passionate about achieving. This may be a new way of thinking for some of your students in that it basically eliminates the excuses and rationalizations prominent in many students' style of thinking. There's a quote from W. H. Murray in *The Scottish Himalaya Expedition* (1951) that is relevant here:

But when I said that nothing had been done I erred in one important matter. We had definitely committed ourselves. . . . Until one is committed, there is hesitancy, the chance to draw back, always ineffectiveness. Concerning all acts of initiative (and creation), there is one elementary truth the ignorance of which kills countless ideas and splendid plans: that the moment one definitely commits oneself, the providence moves too. A whole stream of events issues from the decision, raising in one's favor all manner of unforeseen incidents, meetings and material assistance, which no man could have dreamt would have come his way. I learned a deep respect for one of Goethe's couplets: "Whatever you can do or dream you can, begin it. Boldness has genius, power and magic in it!" (p. 2)

Many school systems today have adopted a committed ''no excuses'' philosophy. On a personal level for a student, embracing this mind-set is tantamount to assuming a fresh sense of self-control of his or her life. As your students exercise self-control to achieve their dream goal, both you and your learners will be amazed at their progress. You will have some that will take an occasional step backward, but with your support they can quickly regain their focus. As their teacher, you can and should model this ''no excuses'' mind-set for your students. In reality, there will be problems to overcome. Give students a problem-solving model to help them with the biggest ones they face. Here's one that we both like:

PROBLEM-SOLVING MODEL FOR STUDENTS

1. Start with a positive attitude.
2. Identify the real problem.
3. State your end goal (and the reward).
4. Identify the resources available.
5. Review the boundaries and limitations.
6. Identify potential paths you could choose.
7. Predict the risks of your chosen path.
8. Choose the strategies to get there.
9. Implement and adapt those strategies as needed.
10. Celebrate success.

Chances are that nobody has ever just laid it out—no one has shown your students a step-by-step system for solving life's problems. Now, the model we just presented is not designed for addressing every single problem on earth. But it applies principles of science, critical thinking, and prediction to achieving goals.

In addition, support and cooperation from peers are also promoters of goal achievement. In studies spanning over eight decades and involving over seventeen thousand young adolescents, the results showed that when adolescents worked cooperatively on goals, peer relationships improved and goals were attained (Roseth, Johnson, & Johnson, 2008). Teenagers can be very social, and positive peer relationships are vitally important to them. As you continue to maintain an atmosphere of cooperation and support in your classroom, the impact on your students' goal achievement will be significant. Cooperation means students are encouraging and helping others to succeed while still working independently on their own goals. There are many possible systems you could devise to facilitate this cooperation. For example, you could establish ''goal buddies'' or small goal groups for encouragement, progress monitoring, and sharing of ideas. As you begin the process of setting and attaining goals with students, consider doing the following:

WHAT YOU CAN DO

- Share quotes and passages about commitment. You might have students memorize a quote as a group activity. Discuss with your students how every accomplishment begins with some type of first step.

- Begin to dispel time myths with your students. A favorite myth among many students is that time can be saved, when in actuality it can only be used more effectively. Remind them that we all have twenty-four hours a day; it's all about prioritizing our time for things that are important to us.

  1. Encourage students to use personal electronic devices for tracking time on task and goal progress. A great resource is www.stickk.com/.

  2. Your students may need a strategy to limit their time on Facebook. Help them set up an "If I get tempted, I will instead . . ." template for themselves.

  3. If students can incorporate a social component into their goal (for example, "Let's both see if we can limit our Facebook time to twenty minutes a day!"), it's usually helpful in achieving that goal.

REMOVING THE ROADBLOCKS

As an educator, you understand the power of setting and achieving goals. You also have witnessed many students who consistently fail to achieve any goal and never really decide to act. They give up because the whole process seems overwhelming and the real or imagined obstacles lure them into inaction. There can be many real obstacles, but there are solutions for overcoming each one. Although it is not intended to be all-inclusive, the chart shown here identifies some common obstacles and possible solutions for goal achievement.

Obstacles to Goal Achievement and Solutions for Overcoming Them

Obstacle	Solution
Lack of seriousness about the goal; lack of passion	Set a compelling goal that evokes positive emotions.
Fear of failure	Expect setbacks and move on; success is often riddled with short-term failures along the way.
Self doubt—uncertainty about one's capability to do long-term, sustained work toward the goal	Identify and focus on personal strengths; maintain daily focus on small steps.
Not meeting a deadline	Examine reasons for not meeting the deadline and set a new one; examine priorities and spend more time on what is the most important.
Lack of organization and focus	Record everything, starting with the big dreams, goals, and daily tasks; keep records in a notebook or on an electronic device and review and revise daily.
Lack of progress	Identify obstacles and address them; continually review progress and implement next steps for achievement.

TO SUM UP

This chapter has departed from traditional goal setting, which promotes smaller goals as a starting point, and promoted a more global initial approach to stir students' excitement and instill a desire to achieve dreams. Many of your students do not see the connection between what they are currently doing in school and what their lives could be like in five, ten, or even fifty years. You have told them in many different ways how important school can be for their future, and yet the message doesn't seem to sink in. That is exactly why a different starting method is suggested here. By using a backward design, students can start visualizing, planning, and establishing personal milestones to achieve their dream goal through consistent small steps. The backwards goal design, once again, works like this: (1) start with a big dream, (2) turn it into long-range goals, (3) set goals with specific outcomes, (4) figure out your intermediate steps, (5) plan what you need to get done this week, but (6) focus on the one thing you can do today.

Achieving goals takes long-term persistence, something many students are lacking when it comes to seeking life success. A goal provides the focus and clarity needed at each step to reach the established milestones. For students, keeping a journal or log of all their dreams, successful steps, and even bumps in the road can be beneficial. This writing can move their mind and spirit forward with purpose and conviction in regard to who they are, what they want, and how to achieve it. A concrete plan that has been put down in writing and shared with a goal group can eliminate procrastination and propel students into needed action. Working toward a big dream is hard work, but writing it down, setting deadlines, making a plan, and taking daily action will lead to success.

After reading this chapter on student goal achievement, you may be asking yourself, "How could I possibly add this to my curriculum? Where would I find the time?" Recognizing the benefits of implementing the backwards goal design for students is the starting place. Next, discuss it with your colleagues and building administration to determine your building's need to teach this concept. With the need established, begin initial planning by determining the grade level or levels for participation, the subject matter for including it, and who will do the teaching. Another possibility is to use any building flex time, such as in homerooms, advisor-advisee periods, or study halls. With careful planning and a goal to make this a reality in your building, it can happen!

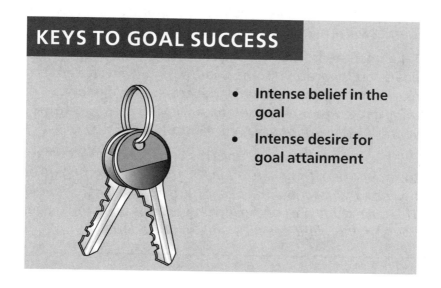

KEYS TO GOAL SUCCESS

- **Intense belief in the goal**
- **Intense desire for goal attainment**

Student Handout: Strategize to Reach Your Goals

- **Be mindful of your dreams and goals**. *Many students consider their dreams for the future to be something apart from their daily activities. They know they are supposed to have dreams and goals, but they place them on a cognitive back burner and don't really work toward achieving them. It's important to recognize the connections between what you do today and your dreams for the future.*

- **Identify the steps necessary to achieve your goals**. *Once you have established the goals—whether they're related to schoolwork, a career, or your personal life—identify the steps you will need to take to move you along. Do some backward planning, starting with the end in mind. To become a doctor, you have to go to medical school. To get into medical school, you need a strong background in biology. It isn't too early to take small steps toward your goals. If you discover along the way that your goals are changing, so much the better that you know earlier rather than later.*

- **Keep a journal to record your progress toward your goals**. *Writing in a journal will keep your dreams alive during those times when it seems like you're never going to get there. A journal will remind you of how far you have come.*

- **Take small steps**. *Examine the milestones for achieving your goals and think about some small, easily achieved steps for reaching these. Acknowledge the achievement of even these small goals. Reward yourself for achieving them, and give yourself a day off for productive work.*

- **Hold fast to your dreams (until it's time to let go)**. *You have to know when it's time to abandon goals. And letting go of goals or dreams shouldn't be a catastrophic event in your life. This is a natural part of the lifelong process of learning about yourself. Be willing to revise, adjust, and adapt.*

REFERENCES

Introduction

Alliance for Excellent Education. (2007). *The crisis in American high schools*. Washington DC: Author. Retrieved from http://www.all4ed.org/whats_at _stake/CrisisInHighSchools.pdf

Levin, H. (2005, October 24–26) The social costs of inadequate education. Paper presented at the 1st annual Teachers College Symposium on Educational Equity, Teachers College, Columbia University, New York, NY. Retrieved from http://www.tc.columbia.edu/i/a/3082_SocialCostsofInadequateEducation.pdf

Chapter One

Alonso-Tapia, J., & Simon, C. (2012). Differences between immigrant and national students in motivational variables and classroom-motivational-climate perception. *Spanish Journal of Psychology*, *15*, 61–74.

Buschkuehl, M., & Jaeggi, S. M. (2010). Improving intelligence: A literature review. *Swiss Medical Weekly*, *140*, 266–272.

Ceci, S., & Williams, W. (1997). Schooling, intelligence, and income. *American Psychologist*, *52*, 1051–1058.

Dell, S. M., & Holmes, A. E. (2012). The effect of a hearing conservation program on adolescents' attitude towards noise. *Noise Health*, *14*(56), 39–44.

Duyme, M., Dumaret, A. C., & Tomkiewicz, S. (1999). How can we boost IQs of ''dull children''? A late adoption study. *Proceedings of the National Academy of Sciences of the United States of America*, *96*, 8790–9784.

Haghani, F., & Sadeghizadeh, A. (2011). Intervention in the learning process of second year medical students. *Journal of Research in Medical Sciences*, *3*, 346–352.

Jaeggi, S. M., Buschkuehl, M., Jonides, J., & Shah, P. (2011). Short- and long-term benefits of cognitive training. *Proceedings of the National Academy of Sciences of the United States of America*, *108*, 10081–10086.

Hattie, J. A. (2009). *Visible Learning*. London, England: Routledge.

Miñano Perez, P., Castejón Costa, J. L., & Gilar Corbí, R. (2012). An explanatory model of academic achievement based on aptitudes, goal orientations, self-concept and learning strategies. *Spanish Journal of Psychology, 15*, 48–60.

Pizzolato, J. E., Brown, E. L., & Kanny, M. A. (2011, Winter). Purpose plus: Supporting youth purpose, control, and academic achievement. *New Directions for Youth Development, 132*, 75–88.

Rodgers, V., & Gilmour, J. (2011). Shaping student nurses' attitudes towards older people through learning and experience. *Nursing Praxis in New Zealand, 27*(3), 13–20.

Salmela-Aro, K., & Tynkkynen, L. (2012, January 31). Gendered pathways in school burnout among adolescents. *Journal of Adolescence, 55*, 929–939.

Tudor-Locke, C., & Lutes, L. (2009). Why do pedometers work? A reflection upon the factors related to successfully increasing physical activity. *Sports Medicine, 39*, 981–993.

Chapter Two

Abel, J. L., & Rissman, E. F. (2012, November 23). Running-induced epigenetic and gene expression changes in the adolescent brain. *International Journal of Developmental Neuroscience*, pii:S0736-5748(12)00585-0. doi:10.1016/j.ijdevneu.2012.11.002

Black, A. E., & Deci, E. L. (2000). The effects of instructors' autonomy support and students' autonomous motivation on learning organic chemistry: A self-determination theory perspective. *Science Education, 84*, 740–756.

Brown, C. L., & Beninger, R. J. (2012). People newly in love are more responsive to positive feedback. *Psychol Reports, 110*, 753–763.

Cage, B., & Smith, J. (2000). The effects of chess instruction on mathematics achievement of Southern, rural, black, secondary students. *Research in the Schools, 1*(7), 19–26.

Dunlop, S. M., & Romer, D. (2010). Adolescent and young adult crash risk: Sensation seeking, substance use propensity and substance use behaviors. *Journal of Adolescent Health, 46*, 90–92.

Gazzaniga, M. (Organizer). (2008). Learning, arts, and the brain: The Dana Consortium report on arts and cognition. (C. Asbury & B. Rich, Eds.). New York, NY: Dana Press. Retrieved from http://www.dana.org/uploadedFiles /News_and_Publications/Special_Publications/Learning,%20Arts%20and %20the%20Brain_ArtsAndCognition_Compl.pdf

Gilman, S. E., Kawachi, I., Fitzmaurice, G. M., & Buka, S. L. (2003). Family disruption in childhood and risk of adult depression. *The American Journal of Psychiatry, 160*, 939–946.

Hattie, J. A. (2011). *Visible learning for teachers*. London, England: Routledge.

Kilgard, M., & Merzenich, M. (1998). Cortical map reorganization enabled by nucleus basalis activity. *Science, 279*, 1714–1718.

Kim, J. Y., Oh, I. H., Lee, E. Y., Choi, K. S., Choe, B. K., Yoon, T. Y., . . . Choi, J. M. (2008) Anthropometric changes in children and adolescents from 1965 to 2005 in Korea. *American Journal of Physical Anthropology, 136*, 230–236.

Klingberg, T., Fernell, E., Olesen, P. J., Johnson, M., Gustafsson, P., Dahlström, K., . . . Westerberg, H. (2005). Computerized training of working memory in children with ADHD—a randomized, controlled trial. *Journal of the American Academy of Child & Adolescent Psychiatry, 44*, 177–186.

Levy, L. M. (2007). Inducing brain growth by pure thought: Can learning and practice change the structure of the cortex? *American Journal of Neuroradiology, 28*, 1836–1837.

Margulies, S. (1991). The effect of chess on reading scores. Retrieved from http://www.uschess.org/scholastic/sc-research.html

Nisbett, R. E., Aronson, J., Blair, C., Dickens, W., Flynn, J., Halpern, D. F., & Turkheimer, E. (2012). Intelligence: New findings and theoretical developments. *American Psychologist, 67*, 130–159.

Norwich, B. (1999). Pupils' reasons for learning and behaving and for not learning and behaving in English and math lessons in a secondary school. *British Journal of Educational Psychology, 69*, 547–569.

Pereira, A. C., Huddleston, D. E., Brickman, A. M., Sosunov, A. A., Hen, R., McKhann, G. M., . . . Small, S. A. (2007). An *in vivo* correlate of exercise-induced neurogenesis in the adult dentate gyrus. *Proceedings of the National Academy of Sciences of the United States of America, 104*, 5638–5643.

Polley, D. B., Steinberg, E. E., & Merzenich, M. M. (2006). Perceptual learning directs auditory cortical map reorganization through top-down influences. *The Journal of Neuroscience, 26*, 4970–4982.

Rutter, M. (2008). Biological implications of gene-environment interaction. *Journal of Abnormal Child Psychology, 36*, 969–975.

Stoolmiller, M. (1998). Correcting estimates of shared environmental variance for range restriction in adoption studies using a truncated multivariate normal model. *Behavior Genetics, 28*, 429–441.

Thompson, P. M., Cannon, T. D., Narr, K. L., van Erp, T., Poutanen, V. P., Huttunen, M., . . . Toga, A. W. (2001). Genetic influences on brain structure. *Nature Neuroscience, 4,* 1253–1258.

Tricomi, E., & Fiez, J. A. (2012). Information content and reward processing in the human striatum during performance of a declarative memory task. *Cognitive, Affective, & Behavioral Neuroscience, 12,* 361–372.

Turkheimer, E. (2000). Three laws of behavior genetics and what they mean. *Current Directions in Psychological Science, 9,* 160–164.

Chapter Three

Bandura, A., Barbaranelli, C., Caprara, G. V., & Pastorelli, C. (1996). Multifaceted impact of self-efficacy beliefs on academic functioning. *Child Development, 67,* 1206–1222.

Bernard, L. C., Mills, M., Swenson, L., & Walsh, R. P. (2005). An evolutionary theory of human motivation. *Genetic, Social, and General Psychology Monographs, 131,* 129–184.

Blackwell, L. S., Trzesniewski, K. H., & Dweck, C. S. (2007). Implicit theories of intelligence predict achievement across an adolescent transition: A longitudinal study and intervention. *Child Development, 78,* 246–263.

DaFonseca, D., Cury, F., Bailly, D., & Rufo, M. (2004). Role of implicit theories in primary school. *Archives of Pediatrics and Adolescent Medicine, 10,* 1225–1229.

Dolan, S. H., Houston, M., & Martin, S. B. (2011). Survey results of the training, nutrition, and mental preparation of triathletes: Practical implications of findings. *Journal of Sports Science, 29,* 1019–1028.

Hoy, W. K., Tarter, C. J., & Hoy, A. W. (2006). Academic optimism of schools: A force for student achievement. *American Educational Research Journal, 43,* 425–446.

Kurniawan, I. T., Guitart-Masip, M., & Dolan, R. J. (2011). Dopamine and effort-based decision making. *Frontiers in Neuroscience, 5,* 81.

LaBode, V. (2011). Text messaging: One step forward for phone companies, one leap backward for adolescence. *International Journal of Adolescent Medicine and Health, 23,* 65–71.

Lupien, S. J., McEwen, B. S., Gunnar, M. R., & Heim, C. (2009). Effects of stress throughout the lifespan on the brain, behaviour and cognition. *Nature Reviews Neuroscience, 10,* 434–445.

Lyons, K. E., & Zelazo, P. D. (2011). Monitoring, metacognition, and executive function: Elucidating the role of self-reflection in the development of self-regulation. *Advances in Child Development and Behavior*, *40*, 379–412.

Mangels, J. A., Butterfield, B., Lamb, J., Good, C., & Dweck, C. S. (2006). Why do beliefs about intelligence influence learning success? A social cognitive neuroscience model. *Social Cognitive and Affective Neuroscience*, *2*, 75–86.

Mosing, M. A., Zietsch, B. P., Shekar, S. N., Wright, M. J., & Martin, N. G. (2009). Genetic and environmental influences on optimism and its relationship to mental and self-rated health: A study of aging twins. *Behavior Genetics*, *39*, 597–604.

Seligman, M.E.P. (2011). Building resilience. *Harvard Business Review*, *89*, 100–106.

Sharot, T., Guitart-Masip, M., Korn, C. W., Chowdhury, R., & Dolan, R. J. (2012). How dopamine enhances an optimism bias in humans. *Current Biology*, *22*, 1477–1481.

Chapter Four

Alloway, T. P., & Alloway, R. G. (2010). Investigating the predictive roles of working memory and IQ in academic attainment. *Journal of Experimental Child Psychology*, *106*, 20–29.

Barrouillet, P., & Lecas, J. F. (1999). Mental models in conditional reasoning and working memory. *Thinking and Reasoning*, *5*, 289–302.

Casey, B., Somerville, L., Gotlib, I., Ayduk, O., Franklin, N., Askren, M., . . . Shoda, Y. (2011). Behavioral and neural correlates of delay of gratification 40 years later. *Proceedings of the National Academy of Sciences of the United States of America*, *108*, 14998–15003.

Checa, P., Rodríguez-Bailón, R., & Rueda, M. (2008). Neurocognitive and temperamental systems of self-regulation and early adolescents' social and academic outcomes. *Mind, Brain, and Education*, *2*, 177–187.

Chermak, G., Tucker, E., & Seikel, A. (2002). Behavioral characteristics of auditory processing disorder and attention-deficit hyperactivity disorder: Predominantly inattentive type. *Journal of the American Academy of Audiology*, *13*, 332–338.

Cutting, L., Matarek, A., Cole, C., Levine, T., & Mahone, E. (2009). Effects of fluency, oral language, and executive function on reading comprehension performance. *Annals of Dyslexia*, *59*, 34–54.

Denckla, M. (2007). Executive function: Binding together the definitions of attention deficit/hyperactivity disorder and learning disabilities. In L. Meltzler

(Ed.), *Executive function in education: From theory to practice* (pp. 5–18). New York, NY: The Guilford Press.

De Smedt, B., Janssen, R., Bouwens, K., Verschaffel, L., Boets, B., & Ghesquière, P. (2009). Working memory and individual differences in mathematics achievement: A longitudinal study from first grade to second grade. *Journal of Experimental Child Psychology, 103*, 186–201.

Don, A., Mateer, C., Streissguth, A., & Kerns, K. (1997). Cognitive deficits in nonretarded adults with fetal alcohol syndrome. *Journal of Learning Disabilities, 30*, 685–693.

Fukuda, K., & Vogel, E. K. (2009). Human variation in overriding attentional capture. *Journal of Neuroscience, 29*, 8726–8733.

Gawrilow, C., Gollwitzer, P., & Oettingen, G. (2011). If-then plans benefit executive functions in children with ADHD. *Journal of Social and Clinical Psychology, 30*, 616–646.

Jaeggi, S. M., Buschkuehl, M., Jonides, J., & Shah, P. (2011). Short- and long-term benefits of cognitive training. *Proceedings of the National Academy of Sciences of the United States of America, 108*, 10081–10086.

Kim, J., Whyte, J., Hart, T., Vaccaro, M., Polansky, M., & Coslett, H. (2005). Executive function as a predictor of inattentive behavior after traumatic brain injury. *Journal of the International Neuropsychological Society, 11*, 434–445.

Lan, X., Legare, C., Ponitz, C., Li, S., & Morrison, F. (2011). Investigating the links between the subcomponents of executive function and academic achievement: A cross-cultural analysis of Chinese and American preschoolers. *Journal of Experimental Child Psychology, 108*, 677–692.

Mischel, W., Shoda, Y., & Rodriguez, M. (1989). Delay of gratification in children. *Science, 244*, 933–938.

Molfese, V. J., Molfese, P. J., Molfese, D. L., Rudasill, K. M., Armstrong, N., & Starkey, G. (2010). Executive function skills of 6 to 8 year olds: Brain and behavioral evidence and implications for school achievement. *Contemporary Educational Psychology, 35*, 116–125.

Mulder, H., Pitchford, N., Hagger, M., & Marlow, N. (2009). Development of executive function and attention in preterm children: A systematic review. *Developmental Neuropsychology, 34*, 393–421.

Rhoades, B., Warren, H., Domitrovich, C., & Greenberg, M. (2011). Examining the link between preschool social-emotional competence and first grade academic achievement: The role of attention skills. *Early Childhood Research Quarterly, 26*, 182–191.

Sarter, M., Gehring, W. J., & Kozak, R. (2006). More attention must be paid: The neurobiology of attentional effort. *Brain Research Reviews, 51*, 145–160.

Stevens, C., Fanning, J., Coch, D., Sanders, L., & Neville, H. (2008). Neural mechanisms of selective auditory attention are enhanced by computerized training: Electrophysiological evidence from language-impaired and typically developing children. *Brain Research, 1205*(5), 55–69.

Temple, E., Deutsch, G., Poldrack, R., Miller, S., Tallal, P., Merzenich, M. & Gabrieli, J. (2003). Neural deficits in children with dyslexia ameliorated by behavioral remediation: Evidence from functional MRI. *Proceedings of the National Academy of Sciences of the United States of America, 100*, 2860–2865.

Thibodeau, L. M., Friel-Patti, S., & Britt, L. (2001). Psychoacoustic performance in children completing Fast ForWord training. *American Journal of Speech-Language Pathology, 10*, 248–257.

Waber, D., DeMoor, C., Forbes, P., Almli, D., Botteron, K., & Leonard, G. (2007). The NIH MRI study of normal brain development: Performance of a population based sample of healthy children aged 6 to 18 years on a neuropsychological battery. *Journal of the International Neuropsychological Society, 13*, 729–746.

Waber, D., Gerber, E., Turcios, V., Wagner, E., & Forbes, P. (2006). Executive functions and performance on high-stakes testing in children from urban schools. *Developmental Neuropsychology, 29*, 457–477.

Willcutt, E., Doyle, A., Nigg, J., Faraone, S., & Pennington, B. (2005). Validity of the executive function theory of attention-deficit/hyperactivity disorder: A meta-analytic review. *Biological Psychiatry, 57*, 1336–1346.

Chapter Five

Andersson, H., & Bergman, L. R. (2011). The role of task persistence in young adolescence for successful educational and occupational attainment in middle adulthood. *Developmental Psychology, 47*, 950–960.

Appleton, J. J., Christenson, S. L., & Furlong, M. J. (2008). Student engagement with school: Critical conceptual and methodological issues of the construct. *Psychology in the Schools, 45*, 369–386.

Black, P., & Wiliam, D. (1998). Assessment and classroom learning. *Assessment in Education: Principles, Policy & Practice, 5*, 7–75.

Carless, D. (2006). Differing perceptions in the feedback process. *Studies in Higher Education, 31*, 219–233.

Duckworth, A. L., & Seligman, M. E. (2005). Self-discipline outdoes IQ in predicting academic performance of adolescents. *Psychological Science, 16*, 939–944.

Fredrickson, B. L., & Losada, M. F. (2005). Positive affect and the complex dynamics of human flourishing. *American Psychologist, 60*, 678–686.

Hattie, J. A. (2003, October 19). Teachers make a difference: What is the research evidence? Paper presented at the Australian Council for Educational Research Annual Conference on Building Teacher Quality, Melbourne, Australia. Retrieved from http://research.acer.edu.au/research_conference_2003

Hattie, J. A. (2010). *Visible learning*. London, England: Routledge.

Hattie, J. A., & Timperley, H. (2007). The power of feedback. *Review of Educational Research, 77*, 81–112.

Ladd, G., & Ladd, D. (2009). Continuity and change in early school engagement: Predictive of children's achievement trajectories from first to eighth grade. *Journal of Educational Psychology, 101*, 190–206.

Marks, H. (2000). Student engagement in instructional activity: Patterns in the elementary, middle, and high school years. *American Educational Research Journal, 37*, 153–184.

Nuthall, G. A. (2005). The cultural myths and realities of classroom teaching and learning: A personal journey. *Teachers College Record, 107*, 895–934.

Rand, K. L. (2009). Hope and optimism: Latent structures and influences on grade expectancy and academic performance. *Journal of Personality, 77*, 231–260.

Reyes, M. R., Brackett, M. A., Rivers, S. E., White, M., & Salovey, P. (2012). Classroom emotional climate, student engagement, and academic achievement. *Journal of Educational Psychology. 104*, 700–712.

Rosenshine, B., & Meister, C. (1994). Reciprocal teaching: A review of the research. *Review of Educational Research, 64*, 479–530.

Shepard, L. A., Flexer, R. J., Hiebert, E. J., Marion, S. F., Mayfield, V., & Weston, T. J. (1996). Effects of introducing classroom performance assessments on student learning. *Educational Measurement Issues and Practice, 15*(3), 7–18.

William, D., Lee, C., Harrison, C., & Black, P. J. (2004). Teachers developing assessment for learning: Impact on student achievement. *Assessment in Education: Principles, Policy & Practice, 11*, 49–65.

Yazzie-Mintz, E. (2010). Indiana University's High School Survey of Student Engagement (HSSSE). Center for Evaluation and Education Policy. Retrieved from http://ceep.indiana.edu/hssse/pdf/HSSSE_2009_Report.pdf

Zimmerman, B. J. (1992). Self-motivation for academic attainment: The role of self-efficacy beliefs and personal goal setting. *American Educational Research Journal, 29*, 663–676.

Chapter Six

Bell, J. T., & Spector, T. D. (2011). A twin approach to unraveling epigenetics. *Trends in Genetics*, *27*, 116–125.

Bouchard, T. J., Jr., (2009). Genetic influence on human intelligence (Spearman's g): How much? *Annals of Human Biology*, *36*, 527–544.

Chan, K. S., & Kitano, M. K. (1986). Demographic characteristics of exceptional Asian students. In M. K. Kitano & P. C. Chinn (Eds.), *Exceptional Asian children and youth* (pp. 1–11). Reston, VA: Council for Exceptional Children.

Colvin, G. (2008). *Talent is overrated: What* really *separates world-class performers from everybody else*. New York, NY: Penguin Group.

Davidson, J., & Davidson, B. (2004). *Genius denied: How to stop wasting our brightest young minds*. New York, NY: Simon & Schuster.

Duncan, G. J., & Magnuson, K. (2005). Can family socioeconomic resources account for racial and ethnic test score gaps? *The Future of Children*, *15*(1), 35–54.

Evans, G. W., & Kim, P. (2012). Childhood poverty and young adults' allostatic load: The mediating role of childhood cumulative risk exposure. *Psychological Science*, *23*, 979–983.

Kalbfleisch, M. (2004). Functional neural anatomy of talent. *The Anatomical Record*, *277*, 21–36.

Kilpatrick, D. G., & Saunders, B. E. (1997). *Prevalence and consequences of child victimization*: *Results from the National Survey of Adolescents*; *Final report*. Charleston: Medical University of South Carolina, National Crime Victims Research and Treatment Center. Retrieved from https://www.ncjrs.gov/pdffiles1/nij/grants/181028.pdf

Lovett, B., & Sparks, R. L. (2011). The identification and performance of gifted students with learning disability diagnoses: A quantitative synthesis. *Journal of Learning Disabilities*. [Epub ahead of print] doi:10.1177/0022219411421810

Mazziotta, J. C., Woods, R., Iacoboni, M., Sicotte, N., Yaden, K., Tran, M., . . . Toga, A. W. (2009). The myth of the normal, average human brain—the ICBM experience: (1) subject screening and eligibility. *Neuroimage*, *44*, 914–922.

National Society for the Gifted & Talented (2012). Giftedness defined—what is gifted and talented? Retrieved from http://www.nsgt.org/articles/index.asp

Nesbitt, R. (2009). *Intelligence and how to get it*. New York, NY: W. W. Norton.

Semrud-Clikeman, M., Walkowiak, J., Wilkinson, A., & Minne, E. P. (2010). Direct and indirect measures of social perception, behavior, and emotional functioning in children with Asperger's disorder, nonverbal learning disability, or ADHD. *Journal of Abnormal Child Psychology, 38*, 509–519.

St. Clair, M. C., Pickles, A., Durkin, K., & Conti-Ramsden, G. (2011). A longitudinal study of behavioral, emotional and social difficulties in individuals with a history of specific language impairment (SLI). *Journal of Communication Disorders, 44*, 186–199.

Tucker-Drob, E. M., Rhemtulla, M., Harden, K. P., Turkheimer, E., & Fask, D. (2011). Emergence of a gene × socioeconomic status interaction on infant mental ability between 10 months and 2 years. *Psychological Science, 22*, 125–133.

Turkheimer, E., Haley, A., Waldron, M., D'Onofrio, B., & Gottesman, I. I. (2003). Socioeconomic status modifies heritability of IQ in young children. *Psychological Science, 14*, 623–628.

Winner, E. (2000). The origins and ends of giftedness. *American Psychologist, 55*, 159–169.

Chapter Seven

Benton, D. (2011). Dehydration influences mood and cognition: A plausible hypothesis? *Nutrients, 3*, 5–73.

Blair, P. S., Humphreys, J. S., Gringras, P., Taheri, S., Scott, N., Emond, A., . . . Fleming, P. J. (2012). Childhood sleep duration and associated demographic characteristics in an English cohort. *Sleep, 35*, 353–360.

Calabrese, R. L., & Schumer, H. (1986). The effects of service activities on adolescent alienation. *Adolescence, 21*, 675–687.

Carskadon, M. A. (2011). Sleep's effects on cognition and learning in adolescence. *Prog Brain Research, 190*, 137–143.

Cian, C., Barraud, P. A., Melin, B., & Raphel, C. (2001). Effects of fluid ingestion on cognitive function after heat stress or exercise-induced dehydration. *International Journal of Psychophysiology, 42*, 243–251.

Cotman, C. W., & Berchtold, N. C. (2002). Exercise: A behavioral intervention to enhance brain health and plasticity. *Trends in Neurosciences, 25*, 295–297.

Erickson, K. I., Miller, D. L., & Roecklein, K. A. (2012). The aging hippocampus: Interactions between exercise, depression, and BDNF. *Neuroscientist, 18*, 82–97.

Erickson, K. I., Voss, M. W., Prakash, R. S., Basak, C., Szabo, A., Chaddock, L., . . . Kamer, A. F. (2011). Exercise training increases size of hippocampus and improves memory. *Proceedings of the National Academy of Sciences of the United States of America, 108*, 3017–3022.

Hamre, B. K., & Pianta, R. C. (2001). Early teacher-child relationships and the trajectory of children's school outcomes through eighth grade. *Child Development*, *72*, 625–638.

Jequier, E., & Constant, F. (2010). Water as an essential nutrient: The physiological basis of hydration. *European Journal of Clinical Nutrition*, *64*, 115–123.

Kannangara, T. S., Lucero, M. J., Gil-Mohapel, J., Dapala R. J., Simkpson, J. M., Christie, B. R., & van Praag, H. (2011). *Neurobiology of Aging*, *32*, 2279–2286.

Khan, T., Powell, L. M., & Wada, R. (2012). Fast food consumption and food prices: Evidence from panel data on 5th and 8th grade children. *Journal of Obesity*, *2012*, article ID: 857697. doi:10.1155/2012/857697

Kleiner, S. M. (1999). Water: An essential but overlooked nutrient. *Journal of the American Dietetic Association*, *99*, 411.

Kleiner, S. M. (2004). The art and science of hydration. *Acta Paediatrica*, *93*, 1557–1558.

Leenaars, C. H., Joosten, R. N., Kramer, M., Post, G., Eggels, L., Wuite, M., . . . Van Someren, E. J. (2012). Spatial reversal learning is robust to total sleep deprivation. *Behavioural Brain Research*, *230*(1), 40–47.

Paluska, S. A., & Schwenk, T. L. (2000). Physical activity and mental health: Current concepts. *Sports Medicine*, *29*, 167–180.

Ratey, J. J., & Loehr, J. E. (2011). The positive impact of physical activity on cognition during adulthood: A review of underlying mechanisms, evidence and recommendations. *Reviews in the Neurosciences*, *22*, 171–185.

Seaman, P. M. (2012). Time for my life now: Early boomer women's anticipation of volunteering in retirement. *Gerontologist*, *52*, 245–254.

Seligman, M. E., Rashid, T., & Parks, A. C. (2006). Positive psychotherapy. *American Psychologist*, *61*, 774–788.

Stillman, T. F., Baumeister, R. F., Lambert, N. M., Crescioni, A. W., Dewall, C. N., & Fincham, F. D. (2009). Alone and without purpose: Life loses meaning following social exclusion. *Journal of Experimental Social Psychology*, *45*, 686–694.

Taki, Y., Hashizume, H., Sassa, Y., Takeuchi, H., Asano, M., Asano, K., & Kawashima, R. (2010). Breakfast staple types affect brain gray matter volume and cognitive function in healthy children. *PLoS One*, *5*, 12.

Wong, G., Dolcos, S., Denkova, E., Morey, R., Wang, L., McCarthy, G., & Dolcos, F. (2012). Brain imaging investigation of the impairing effect of emotion on cognition. *Journal of Visualized Experiments*, *60*, e2434. doi:10.3791/2434

Wycherley, T. P., Noakes, M., Clifton, P. M., Cleanthous, X., Keogh, J. B., & Brinkworth, G. D. (2010). Timing of protein ingestion relative to resistance exercise training does not influence body composition, energy expenditure, glycaemic control or cardiometabolic risk factors in a hypocaloric, high protein diet in patients with type 2 diabetes. *Diabetes, Obesity, and Metabolism, 12,* 1097–1105.

Chapter Eight

DeWall, C. N., Baumeister, R. F., Mead, N. L., & Vohs, K. D. (2011). How leaders self-regulate their task performance: Evidence that power promotes diligence, depletion, and disdain. *Journal of Personality and Social Psychology, 100,* 47–65.

Dijksterhuis, A., & Aarts, H. (2010). Goals, attention, and (un)consciousness. *Annual Review of Psychology, 61,* 467–490.

Elliott, E. S., & Dweck, C. S. (1988). Goals: An approach to motivation and achievement. *Journal of Personality and Social Psychology, 54,* 5–12.

Klein, H. J., Wesson, M. J., Hollenbeck, J. R., & Alge, B. J. (1999). Goal commitment and the goal-setting process: Conceptual clarification and empirical synthesis. *Journal of Applied Psychology, 84,* 885–896.

Masicampo, E. J., & Baumeister, R. F. (2011). Consider it done! Plan making can eliminate the cognitive effects of unfilled goals. *Journal of Personality and Social Psychology, 101,* 667–683.

Mischel, W., Shoda, Y., & Rodriquez, M. I. (1989). Delay of gratification in children. *Science, 244,* 933–938.

Murray, W. H. (1951). *The Scottish Himalayan expedition.* London, England: Dent.

Rabin, L. A., Fogel, J., & Nutter-Upham, K. E. (2011). Academic procrastination in college students: The role of self-reported executive function. *Journal of Clinical & Experimental Neuropsychology, 33,* 344–357.

Roseth, C. J., Johnson, D. W., & Johnson, R. T. (2008). Promoting early adolescents' achievement and peer relationships: The effects of cooperative, competitive, and individualistic goal structures. *Psychological Bulletin, 134,* 223–246.

Teti, M., Martin, A. E., Ranade, R., Massie, J., Malebranche, D. J., Tschann, J. M., & Bowleg, L. (2012). ''I'm a keep rising. I'm a keep going forward, regardless'': Exploring black men's resilience amid sociostructural challenges and stressors. *Quality Health Research Journal, 22,* 524–533.

Zimmerman, B. J., Bandura, A., & Martinez-Pons, M. (1992). Self-motivation for academic attainment: The role of self-efficacy beliefs and personal goal setting. *American Educational Research Journal, 29,* 663–676.

Index